A PRIMER ON POWER

DISCOVERING THE DYNAMIC MINISTRY OF THE HOLY SPIRIT

Scott Camp

Franklin Publishing
GREENVILLE, TEXAS

Kelly Carr / Franklin Publishing
102 Edgewood Dr.
Greenville, Texas 75402
www.FranklinPublishing.org

Ordering Information:
Quantity sales. Special discounts are available on quantity purchases by corporations, associations, conventions, and churches. For details, contact the "Special Sales Department" at the address above.

Except where otherwise indicated, all Scripture quotations in this book are from the New American Standard Bible 1960, 1962, 1963, 1968, 1971, 1972, 1973, 1975, 1977, and 1995 by the Lockman Foundation, and are used by permission.

Printed in the United States of America by Franklin Publishing, 2016

A Primer On Power: Discovering The Dynamic Ministry Of The Holy Spirit / Scott Camp. —1st ed.

All rights reserved.
ISBN: 0-9666464-3-6
ISBN-13: 978-0-9666464-3-6

Testimonials

Scott Camp is a man of God. His book on the matchless experience with the Holy Spirit is essential for all believers. His sound theology is mixed with his amazing personal testimony. The impact to you as you read will bring permanent change and lasting fruit!
Dr Larry Lea, Best Selling Author, *Could You Not Tarry One Hour?*

In this practical and biblically sound resource, Scott Camp offers challenge and inspiration to every believer desiring the power of the Holy Spirit in everyday life.
Kermit Bridges, D.Min., President, SAGU

Scott Camp has hit on the one great need for a church under siege from without and beset by decay within--the power of the Holy Spirit! If you're weary of watching the body of Christ retreat in defeat and fade away into irrelevance, this book contains the pearl you've been looking for.
Dr. Jeff Wickwire, Founder/Sr. Pastor, Turning Point Church, Ft Worth, TX, Radio Host of LifeTalk Radio

Scott Camp is an authentic Ephesians 4 Evangelist. He fulfills this calling by leading many to a saving knowledge of Christ and equipping the global and local Church for effective evangelism and thoughtful discipleship. Scott is a rare gift to the world, uniting Pentecostal passion for the outreach with intellectual depth and personal winsomeness.

Scott's new Book, *A Primer on Power* is at once personal testimony, excellent exhortation for God's people to rely on the Spirit and careful biblical-theological reflection of Spirit-baptism, speaking in tongues and the importance of all the gifts and expression of the Spirit available for believers partnering with God in the mission of reconciliation.

Scott graciously challenges non-Pentecostal Evangelicals to awaken from ossified philosophies and rationalistic snares and welcome the fullness of the Spirit. He also refuses to capitulate to the fads and sometimes shallow theology of popular Pentecostal and Charismatic personalities. There is something in this book for everyone. I recommend this as a biblical wake-up call for a slumbering Western church.

Dr. Charlie Self, Professor of Church History, The Assemblies of God Theological Seminary, Co-founder, *The Discipleship Dynamics Assessment* ™

Easy to read and digest. Here, Dr. Camp makes the Holy Spirit the object of his attention, and shares biblical and practical insights that are helpful and hopeful. Pleased to commend.

Dr. Jeffrey L. Seif, The King's University, Southlake, TX

Scott Camp has brought his considerable skills as a gifted preacher of God's Word to the printed page in order to help faithful men and women learn more about the person and work of the Holy Spirit. One need not agree with all aspects of Camp's proposals to find much in this volume that will be helpful, edifying, and encouraging. I trust that God will use this book to empower individual believers and to strengthen congregations for the advancement of the gospel in this country and around the globe.

David S. Dockery, President, Trinity International University

Every biblically-informed believer in Jesus affirms the need of a Spirit-empowered life. Scott Camp has provided a great service for every follower of Jesus with the publication of *A Primer on Power*. This thoroughly biblical portrayal of the Spirit's person and work will inform you and help equip you as Christ's witness and ambassador. Dr. Camp is warm and practical in every chapter. He combines fidelity to Scripture, heartwarming insights, and clear steps toward a life of spiritual joy, power, and fruitfulness. You will want to read this book several times and purchase copies for your friends.

This is awesome, Scott! I know the Spirit Himself will breathe on this book and use it to bring many into His fullness. Thanks for writing it.
David Shibley, Founder, Global Advance

Scott Camp is a Biblical scholar and a New Testament evangelist, which uniquely qualifies him to write 'A Primer on Power.' He lays bare the western church's need for fresh empowerment from the Holy Spirit. May we heed his admonition.
Richard Exley Author, *Man of Valor, When You Lose Someone You Love*, **and** *Deliver Me*

Scott Camp is a man saved from the deepest of sinful living to a life in Jesus Christ. Scott loves Jesus! I know his life. The fullness of God's Spirit flows through him He has a solid understanding of the work and power of the Holy Spirit. Anyone reading this book will have a clear understanding of the baptism in the Holy Spirit. Great read!
Dr Morris Sheets Founding Pastor, Hillcrest Church, in Dallas, TX

Scott Camp is a uniquely brilliant and highly gifted evangelist. Having seen thousands upon thousands receive Jesus as Lord and Savior in his work, his demand for a Spirit-filled life and ministry rings with a clarity that cannot be ignored. This succinct primer is replete with his undeniable life experiences in the power of the Holy Spirit and a clear guide for any individual seeking to enter the anointing, giftings, blessings and remarkable joy which is the life in the Holy Spirit. I believe this work will be become a handbook to lead Christians into the power of the Holy Spirit which will result in the salvation of unlimited numbers of precious individuals around the globe.

Dr Richard Hogue Senior Pastor, City Church Oklahoma City, OK. Author, *The Jesus Touch*

Scott Camp has written a book that is part testimony and part apologetic. He has experienced what he writes about and he has built biblical foundations for his spiritual journey that can benefit every serious follower of Jesus. His experience as an evangelist was in response to a divine call from God to proclaim the Gospel. But that obedience drove him to realize that his considerable skill at effective communication wasn't enough for him to faithfully follow that calling from God.

Ultimately Scott encountered the guarantee of Pentecost: which is simply that the Jesus whose ministry is authoritatively recorded in the Gospels is the Jesus who is doing the exact same things in the 21st century. Is it any wonder that Jesus would continue His ministry today and want to empower His followers with that same Holy Spirit?

Simple to read but never simplistic; *A Primer on Power* is a book that will provide clarity for followers of Jesus hungry for a deeper and more powerful encounter with God. Scott Camp provides biblical foundations that are accessible and understandable for all Christians serious about effective ministry. Holy Spirit power is a non-negotiable for effective ministry in the 21st century and Scott Camp confidently bears witness to the necessity of a personal Pentecost for every believer today.

Byron D. Klaus, President Assemblies of God Theological Seminary (1999-2015)

I dare any Christian who has ever asked, "Is this all there is to it, or is there more," to read this book with an open heart and mind. In this brief primer readers will find the real story of a man who came to a summons to experience the supernatural power of a Spirit-filled life and stepped over the edge. Scott Camp makes no apologies for his journey, and he certainly paid a dear price in the networks of church ecclesiology and ministry bureaucracy for his choice. Like Moses, he walked away from a promising career as a soaring denominational evangelist to become a servant of God who wanted more to receive the praises of God rather than the praises of men. *A Primer on Power* is a book about hunger, courage, and faith that results in the power of God that most people read about but never experience for themselves.

Pastor Ron Meador, Bethel Church Duncan, Oklahoma

In his very user friendly book, *A Primer on Power*, not only does Dr. Scott Camp diagnose the powerlessness of the modern church, but he offers a simple, practical and complete solution to the lack of the supernatural in the midst of Western Christianity. This book is a must read for all believers, especially those who are young in the faith and desire more POWER with God in their personal experience!

Dr. Dwain Miller, Senior Pastor of Cross Life Church, El Dorado, AR

Scott Camp's little book is an incredible melding of sophisticated Biblical scholarship with spirit-filled insight and engaging story-telling. It diagnoses without hesitation what is wrong with the church today and prescribes exactly what is required.

Carl Raschke, Professor of Religious Studies, University of Denver, Author, *GloboChrist*

Scott Camp has done us all a favor with his book, *A Primer on Power*! For Pentecostals and Charismatics, he provides us with scholarly, line-upon-line in Scripture proofs that God wants *everyone* to be baptized in the Holy Spirit AND to experience all the manifestations of the Holy Spirit ever offered to The Church. For those who have thought those gifts and experiences ended with the Apostles, those Biblical proofs are persuasive for our *head*, while his own story of moving into the things of the Spirit can persuade our *heart* to receive *all* that God has for us today!
Jerry McQuay, Senior Pastor, Christian Life Center, Tinley Park, IL

For many believers, the Holy Spirit is like the weird uncle at a family gathering. Everyone knows he's part of the family, but no one knows how he got there, or even what purpose he serves. In Scott's new book, he takes the reader on a deep journey into experiencing how vital, unique and precious the work of the Spirit is in each of our lives.
Dr. David Edwards, Pastor of Discipleship at Church Project, Author and Speaker

Dr. Scott Camp is a powerful evangelist and, in this book, Scott shares his perspective on tapping into God's power.
Dr. Mike Cramer Founder, Power For Living Ministry, Lead Pastor, New Life Church, Author, *Power Moments*.

According to tradition, Paul was a small man, short of stature and unimpressive in appearance. Yet, in the kingdom of God he was an apostolic giant. Dr. Scott Camp refers to his new work on the Holy Spirit a "little book" but like the famed apostle it is big with truth and anointing. Scott shares his own personal encounter with the "Spirit which is from God," but this book does not promote an extra-biblical experience in search of an affirming doctrine. To the contrary, Scott lays a solid New Testament foundation for the baptism in the Holy

Spirit and then encourages all believers to experience this biblical gift. Every Christian should read *A Primer on Power* with expectancy, anticipating more of God in their lives.
Dr Larry Martin, Evangelist, Educator, Author

Scott Camp is an anointed preacher of the gospel who is ablaze with the love and power of God's Spirit as we all should be. His testimony and explorations of God's Word in this volume will bless many. May his tribe increase!
Larry Hart, PhD, Professor of Theology, Graduate School of Theology and Ministry, Oral Roberts University, Tulsa, OK

Scott Camp is very excited about the Holy Spirit! And he should be! Everyone born again by the Spirit of God is indwelt by the Spirit. Scott celebrates this great truth, but he also emphasizes the absolute necessity of the Spirit's power in the life and ministry of every believer. Not every person indwelt by the Spirit experiences the dynamic—the fullness, the energy, the control, the power—of the Spirit. Scott longs for God's people to enter into the life of the Spirit, and those who read his book will come away with that same longing. While not everyone, on every scripture passage or theological matter discussed in this book, will arrive at the same conclusions as Scott, all will benefit greatly by reading this book with an open mind and heart. As Scott stresses, for the church of Christ to stumble along with only a mental assent to the doctrine of the Spirit is to ignore and disobey the very One whom Christ sent at Pentecost to empower mightily every child of God for the work of God's kingdom. The Spirit of the Lord—the Spirit of holiness and might—will surely come in his fullness to everyone who sincerely cries out for the passion and fire of God's purity and power. He will not ignore the cries of his beloved!
Robert V. Rakestraw, Ph.D. Professor of Theology Emeritus, Bethel Seminary Founder and Director, Grace Quest Ministries

Scott Camp is a dear friend, church leader, educator and evangelist. He carries a great burden and a tremendous gift to reconcile the world to God through relationship with Jesus Christ. He and his teachings have greatly impacted me and the lives of countless thousands around the world. Today the world desperately needs a manifestation of God's power. God desires to use His church the vehicle for the expression of His eternal ability. This book is wonderful tool that will help introduce, inspire and release that power in the life of the believer.
Shane Warren, Lead Pastor of The Assembly, West Monroe, La.

Scott Camp's book is a heartwarming invitation to open the door of the church wide to the power of the Holy Spirit and to the full spectrum of spiritual gifts that can enter as a result. He urges us all on page after page not to be afraid of what the Holy Spirit can do in powerful witness to Christ once we gain the courage to yield.
Frank D. Macchia, D.Theol., D.D., Professor of Christian Theology, Vanguard University

Scott Camp is an effective evangelist who has drawn thousands into the gospel net. He also has a secret. His ministry shifted into a higher gear after he had a dynamic encounter with the Holy Spirit. In this book, part biography and part theology, Scott tells his story and shares his secret, but most of all encourages his readers to discover the power of the Holy Spirit for themselves.
R. Alan Streett, PhD Senior Research Professor of Biblical Theology, Criswell College, Dallas, Texas

Many Bible-believing Christians come from churches that do not believe the full scope of the spiritual gifts the New Testament talks about is suppose to last beyond the time of the apostles. Scott Camp writes as someone who used to hold such

views himself, and has a pastoral heart especially for such persons who are willing to take another look at what the Bible says about the person and work of the Holy Spirit and who are open to being touched and revived afresh by the Spirit today.
Amos Yong, Fuller Theological Seminary, Author, *Who Is the Holy Spirit? A Walk with the Apostles*

I read Dr. Scott Camp's book on the work of the Spirit with great interest. In my opinion, this book tackles some of the most frequently asked questions about the work of the Spirit in the life of the believer and the local church. His approach is direct, insightful, and Biblically sound. In my opinion, this book is a must read for every pastor, church leader, and child of God.
Don Nordin, Lead Pastor, CT Church Houston TX, President & CEO, Global Ministries Network, Author, *The Audacity of Prayer*

My friend, Scott Camp, has written a powerful and timely message for the church in America. My own faith was stirred as I read his story and his exposition of Scripture. I highly recommend this book to every Christian leader and every believer who is tired of church as usual and hungers for the Christianity of those earliest followers of Jesus whom we read about in the Book of Acts.
Dr. Eddie L. Hyatt, Author and Bible Teacher

Here is a clarion call to receive all that the Spirit of God has for the Body of Christ in order to become and accomplish the will of the Father. Scott Camp offers a compelling personal testimony and exposition of Scripture for everyone who calls on the name of the Lord to receive the empowerment that is theirs in the Holy Spirit.
Rev. Rick Wadholm Jr., V.P. of Academics, Trinity Bible College & Graduate School, Ellendale, ND

Scott is one of the premier evangelists of our time. His love and devotion to His Lord shines through every page. His desire to embrace a limitless God, no matter the personal cost is an exhortation to every preacher of our day. We live in a world steeped in sin, which desperately needs preachers who not only expound upon the truths of God's Word, but embrace the power, the unction that brings God's Word alive within ones heart. Scott Camp's life is a powerful witness to what it means to be a Spirit filled, Spirit led preacher!
George Neau, Chancellor SUM Bible College & Theological Seminary

Dr. Scott's Camp's book provides us with a much-needed compass for understanding the Holy Spirit's work in eroding the divisions that separate us, especially in the Church. His insightful analysis of Pentecost points us in the direction of becoming a truly missional church by helping us to comprehend the Holy Spirit's agenda in baptizing us. A rare combination of biblical scholarship, practical wisdom and living testimony, this book convincingly reminds us that the Holy Spirit has more in store for us than we ever dreamed, and we don't have to wait until we get to heaven to receive it. I highly recommend this book.
Dr. Christena Cleveland, Associate Professor of the Practice of Reconciliation at Duke Divinity School and Author, *Disunity in Christ: Uncovering the Hidden Forces that Divide Us*

Scott Camp's remarkable work of evangelism in this 21st century goes beyond the borders of human desire and endeavor to preach the good news to the ends of the earth. His work is filled with the love and power of God as revealed by the Holy Spirit who is promised to "all flesh" in Joel 2:28. Thus, Camp's book, *A Primer on Power*, explains the Power behind his powerful ministry that brings hundreds of souls into the Kingdom of Christ every day and week. This book succinctly explains the function and nature of the Holy Spirit, underscores the indispensability of the infilling of the Holy Spirit based on the Bible, captures Camp's walk and relationship with the person of the Holy Spirit, and demonstrates the need and relevance of the Holy Spirit to the body of Christ that comprises of men, women, youth and children of all language, tribe and nation as they live and work in these apocalyptic times.

Sheba K. George, Ph.D., Ed.D., Founder and Superintendent, Newman International Academy

The results of Evangelist Scott Camp's ministry are self-evident and undeniable in his numerous, public evangelistic meetings and campaigns in churches and auditoriums across America. Hundreds and thousands of individuals are accepting Jesus Christ as their personal Savior, being healed by the power of Jesus Christ and receiving the power of the Holy Spirit for ministry in their own lives. The results of Scott's ministry are authentically of the same quality and character as those that Luke the Evangelist records of the First Century Church in the Acts of the Apostles. Why are these undeniable outcomes accompany his ministry? Scott tells us why in this inspiring, personal account of how God has supernatural led him from a jail cell into one of the most amazing and outstanding ministries of our times!

John W. Wyckoff, Ph.D., Professor of Bible and Theology, Southwestern Assemblies of God University, Waxahachie, TX

Writing from an experience of the dynamic impact of the Holy Spirit's power both on personal life and ministry, Scott Camp writes on how the church today could have the kind of Kingdom impact the early church had on her community as recorded in the Book of Acts. Scott contends that the ministry of the church is unalterably linked to the work and ministry of the Holy Spirit without which the church has no power and

the Christian has no victory. I agree with Scott on this profound truth so well articulated. *A Primer on Power* is a must read for all Christians, pastors, church workers, and missionaries who share the burden of world evangelization and community transformation through the power of the Holy Spirit.
Rev. Dr. Paul Frimpong-Manso, General Superintendent, Assemblies of God, Ghana

Scott Camp has written a helpful book for those interested in the presence, power and gifts of the Holy Spirit.
Dr Ken Archer, Professor of Theology and Pentecostal Studies, Southeastern University, Lakeland, FL

Scott Camp's, *A Primer on Power*, introduces the reader to the Holy Spirit and the Pentecostal baptism. Challenging an Evangelicalism that he sees as deficient in power and surviving on "life supports," Camp weaves together biblical commentary, personal testimony, and theological musings to promote a Spirit-empowered life and church. According to Camp, the Pentecostal baptism transforms and empower personal lives as well as exposes and confronts racism as well as sexism.
Dr David Daniels, Professor of Church History, McCormick Theological Seminary, Bishop COGIC

"But you will receive power when the Holy Spirit comes on you; and you will be my witnesses in Jerusalem, and in all Judea and Samaria, and to the ends of the earth."

Acts 1:8 (NIV)

Contents

Foreword

What a great Kingdom service Scott Camp has given us in his scholarly and passionate book on the Holy Spirit. Contained in this very readable work is liberating truth that will set all who read it on the journey to fullness. Here he unfolds the missing element in the traditional as well as the contemporary church. While acknowledging the excesses Scott affirms the need and relevance for all the spiritual gifts to be unleashed in the church. This is not a fad for Scott. It is the inevitable outgrowth of a strong belief in Biblical infallibility and authority. I commend this work to all of Gods people. Pastors will find it rich in truth and the laymen will enjoy its simplicity.

Pastor Ron Phillips
Abbas House / Central Baptist Church
Chattanooga, Tennessee

Preface

I am writing this little book or "primer" in the hope that it will create within the hearts of all who read it a hunger for a deeper experience with the Holy Spirit. The Holy Spirit is God. He is the third member of what Christians have traditionally referred to as the Trinity. The Holy Spirit is not the Father or the Son, yet He is God. He is no less God than the Father or the Son and yet His Person and Work have often been ignored. The Holy Spirit is also a person. He is not a "force" and should never be referred to in anything less than personal terms. To do so must be tremendously grievous to Him.

I am writing this book as an orthodox and Evangelical Christian who has had a definite experience of empowerment with the Holy Spirit. I am unapologetically Charismatic. I believe in an experience of empowerment subsequent to regeneration which has commonly been referred to as the baptism of the Holy Spirit. The purpose of this book is to introduce this subject in the hopes that my readers may enter into this fullness of the life of the Spirit and His ministry gifts.

I realize that many of my readers may not share my view of the work of the Spirit. But I think all of us will admit that something is desperately wrong with the Western Church. Much of my thinking about this issue has been shaped by my travels to Africa over the past 15 years. I have seen firsthand the explosive growth of Charismatic Christianity in the various nations of this vibrant continent. Most of this growth, particularly the conversion of Muslims, can be directly attributed to the supernatural power of the Holy Spirit. The deaf are hearing, the blind seeing, the lame are walking and yes, the dead are being raised. God is pouring out His power in ways reminiscent of the Book of Acts.

We desperately need a revival in the West. We need the power of the Holy Spirit. This move of the Spirit is our only hope. I am asking you to read this little book carefully and prayerfully and to be open to the truth that God may well be calling you into a deeper experience with the Spirit.

A word of warning: experiencing the power of God is costly. But the result is well worth the price!

Scott Camp
March 2016, Arlington, Texas

Acknowledgements

Several people have played key roles in the production of this "little book." Almost 30 years ago, a young atheist was brought to one of our Crusades by some teenage girls. He left a believer in Christ and subsequently became a pastor and journalist. Through the miracle of Facebook, Scott Rutherford and I reconnected after almost 25 years. Scott has been a constant source of encouragement in my new writing ministry. He has helped me shape this book for your enjoyment. Thank you Scott.

I wish to thank Dr. Rick Wadholm, Academic Dean at Trinity Bible College for his helpful critique of the manuscript along with my long time research assistant, recent Yale Divinity School graduate and son in the ministry, John Cleveland, for lending his considerable skills in shaping this text. Thanks to one of my top SUM.edu students, Kristene O'Dell, for writing the discussion questions at the end of the chapters.

My father in the things of the Spirit, Dr Richard Hogue, has helped me think through the theology of "Power." He and Marilyn have been a blessing beyond words to Gina and me for almost 30 years. Thanks "Dad."

I want to acknowledge Dr. Doug Oss, my primary Professor in my doctoral work at AGTS in Springfield, MO. It was Doug's emphasis on Biblical vs. Systematic Theology which opened my mind to thinking about the ministry of the Spirit from Luke's uniquely "charismatic" perspective. Thanks Doug.

Finally I want to thank my sister, best friend, partner in ministry and love of my life, my wife, Gina. We have walked this path together, side by side, from young Southern Baptist Evangelists to People of the Spirit. God has blessed us with four beautiful and brilliant children: Sarah, Dillon, Joshua and Madison. They are the fruit of our love.

"A major factor in the current revival in the Third World-by some estimates, up to 70 percent of it-is intimately connected to signs and wonders as expressions of the love of the Christian Father-God, the lordship of His Son, and the power of His Spirit and His Kingdom. A manifestation of the supernatural power of God through healings, demonic deliverances, and the prophetic are central to what is going on today."

Philosopher JP Moreland in *The Kingdom Triangle*

CHAPTER ONE

The Essential Holy Spirit

Wind, Fire, Dove. These are words and images used in the New Testament to describe the ministry of the Holy Spirit. But the word I like the most is power! This is a book about power. More specifically, this is a book about the power of the Holy Spirit and how this power dramatically impacted both my personal life and ministry. It is a book written to help you and your church discover the dynamic ministry of the Holy Spirit. So, buckle up and get ready to learn about and experience in a new way the power of the Holy Spirit!

According to LifeWay Research, 78% of the Evangelical churches in the U.S. have plateaued or are in decline. Of the 22% which are growing, half are growing through transfers of membership.[1] While Jesus has called us to be "fishers of men," we are content to be "keepers of the aquarium." Few churches are having the kind of Kingdom impact on their communities that we read about in The Book of Acts. Sadly, the vast majority of churches in the US are on "life support" trying to keep the bills paid and the doors open. There is no doubt that the Church needs the power of God now more than ever. Fortunately, the power of God is as available as ever. The question is, "Do we earnestly desire the Spirit's power?"

There are places around the world where Christians are desperate for the power of God. They aggressively seek God's presence and power and realize that without His supernatural strength (divine enablement) they are helpless to do the work of God. Each year I spend several weeks in the Majority World. In nations on the continent of Africa, I have preached in humble buildings filled with people who hunger and thirst for the power of God. People crowd these buildings, flowing into the streets, leaning through the windows in hope of being touched by the Holy Spirit. These people and churches are typically referred to as "charismatic" or Pentecostal. Their gatherings are characterized by power! There are currently over 500 million of these believers in the earth, second only to Roman Catholics in sheer numerical strength.[2] They are by far the fastest growing segment of the church.

Each time I minister in such contexts, my own faith is stretched to believe God for demonstrations of His power. In Africa, the physical needs of the people are overwhelming. There are no hospitals, doctors or nurses, and many remote villages lack the basic medical supplies found in a typical first-aid kit. When a preacher brings the Good News of the Kingdom of God, the expectation of the people is that there will be powerful healings and exorcisms to rid God's people of debilitating pain and mental or emotional illnesses. Time and again, I have prayed, "Lord I believe! Help my unbelief." It is amazing what God does when we step out in childlike faith and trust Him for the miraculous. I have personally witnessed God heal many different kinds of illnesses as an expression of His love for these precious people. In Kampala, Uganda dozens of Muslims were converted to Christ after seeing one of their friends healed of lameness. Our God is all-powerful and He delights in healing the sick. Father, increase our faith!

By way of contrast, I have also stood in some of the magnificent cathedrals in Europe. At one time, these great edifices were at the center of genuine demonstrations of the power of God. Today they are museums. There are no people and there is no power!

It seems that the American church often assumes that money, buildings, programs, celebrity preachers or a myriad of other factors are the "secret sauce" needed to impact the community. We have all of these in abundance and yet our nation is increasingly pagan. What is the answer?

I want to suggest that the mission of the church is unalterably linked to the work and ministry of the Holy Spirit. Without His ministry, the church has no power and the Christian has no victory. It is the presence of the Spirit which sets men and women apart from the rest of creation as the ones uniquely made in the image of God, the objects of His love, and the instruments through whom He intends to establish His will on the earth. It is through the work of the Spirit that we are restored as full image bearers, thereby placing inestimable worth and value on the new creation and releasing the power and authority of heaven into the life of each Christian. It is the ministry of the Spirit which brings broken, lost, sinful persons fully into the family of God as His beloved children. It is the ministry of the Spirit which equips and releases the sons and daughters of God into the global work of redemption, bringing His saving love and forgiveness to each person in the world. Regrettably, this is not happening as powerfully as God intends.

Our world is a mess, and the crisis has nothing to do with the things we typically blame. The problem is not political. Some of the most powerful and productive days of the church occurred during the years in which the Roman Emperor Nero, one of the most vile, hedonistic and wicked rulers of all time, attempted to destroy the church. He persecuted the church on an unprecedented level. Christians were crucified, burned alive and used as human torches to light his gardens. These Spirit-empowered believers were run through with swords and fed to the lions in the Roman Coliseum. The blood of these martyrs became the seed of the church. The problem in the church goes beyond politics, the economy or any social ill. The problem is not the success of competing world religions such as Islam. When the Church was birthed, the world was filled with hundreds of religions which dominated the Greco-Roman world. Yet the church possessed a remarkable earth-shaking power which ultimately transformed the empire. The early disciples traversed the known world, preached and demonstrated the Gospel of the Kingdom in the power of the

Holy Spirit. This power validated the message of Jesus and brought thousands into the Kingdom of God.

So, if the problem is not political, economic, societal or religious, what is it?

> *THE PROBLEM TODAY IS A LACK OF POWER IN THE CHURCH CAUSED BY IGNORANCE AND THE SUBTLE REJECTION OF THE MINISTRY OF THE HOLY SPIRIT.*

The problem is a lack of power in the church caused by ignorance and the subtle rejection of the ministry of the Holy Spirit. If the work of the Spirit is rejected or ignored in the church, there will be a lack of power and victory in the life of the average Christian even though he or she may attend church every Sunday.

The fact that the church is devoid of the power of God is apparent. Sobering statistics demonstrate that moral and ethical issues such as teenage pregnancy, divorce, racism, adultery, alcohol and drug abuse, sexism, pornography addiction and a host of other dysfunctional beliefs and behaviors are as rampant inside the Church as they are in the unchurched world.[3]

Facing the Real Problem

The real problem is an absence of power in the church and in the lives of individual Christians caused by a lack of understanding of the Person and, in many cases, a rejection of the power and ministry gifts of the Holy

Spirit. I have heard it said that if the sin of the Old Testament was an ignorance and rejection of God the Father and if the problem in the New Testament was an ignorance and rejection of God the Son, Jesus (by His own people), then surely our sin today, is an ignorance of – and in many cases, a rejection of – God the Holy Spirit.

This Must Stop!

The power of the Holy Spirit is not to be feared, not to be rejected and not to be limited to a select number of Christians. The Holy Spirit is a supernatural Person, equal in the Godhead with the Father and the Son. The Spirit is not a force nor is He an impersonal influence floating about the creation. He is a Divine Being who can be experienced and known personally. Christianity is not primarily a philosophy, ideology, or religious ritual. Rather, Christianity is Christ alive in us through the presence of the Spirit. As Christians, we have the joy of knowing God as Father, Son and Spirit.

Through the Spirit, God speaks to us, placing a strong demand upon us to reject an outward, superficial relationship with the mere idea of the Holy Spirit and settle for nothing less than the absolute experience of His person and power as He makes Jesus real in and through our lives. After all, the Holy Spirit is not primarily a doctrine to be discussed; rather He is a Person we can know intimately. We can feel His presence and experience His power. For the apostle Paul (who wrote much on the Spirit) and his churches "the Spirit is not only the absolute key to their understanding of Christian life—from beginning to end—but above all else the Spirit was experienced, and experienced in ways that were essentially powerful and visible."[4]

If you have received Jesus as Lord and Savior, the Holy Spirit is present in your life. In fact, it is impossible to be a Christian and not to be in-dwelt by the Holy Spirit. If the Holy Spirit is not in your life, you are not a Christian. "If anyone does not have the Spirit of Christ, he is not of Christ" (Rom. 9:8).

Born Again

One of the most remarkable things Jesus ever said occurred as He talked to a man named Nicodemus. He totally surprised Nicodemus when he declared, "You must be born again" (John 3:3). In order to explain what He meant, Jesus continued, "That which is born of the flesh is flesh, and that which is born of the Spirit is spirit" (John 3:6). What did He mean by the expression "born of the Spirit?"

Because of sin, (both personal disobedience to God's law and a sin nature inherited from your first parents Adam and Eve) your spirit was dead (Eph. 2:1). The moment you received Jesus as Lord and Savior, the Holy Spirit entered your life and your spirit came alive. You were "born again" because the Holy Spirit came to live inside of your dead spirit as you confessed Jesus Christ as Lord. The breath of God blew across your dead spirit and like air coming into your lungs; the Spirit of God came to live in your spirit. When you accepted Jesus, asking Him to come live in your heart (Eph. 3:17), that's exactly what happened! The Holy Spirit, the invisible Jesus, came to live in your spirit and you were born from above!

At that moment, you were saved. You were regenerated and became a full son or daughter of God (Gal. 4:6). Unfortunately, this is where the vast majority of believers stop. Seemingly, many of God's people only want to know that they are saved and will get to go to heaven when they die. But in the meantime, they are living in defeat, frustration, sitting on their "blessed assurance" while waiting for the rapture bus to swoop down out of heaven and take them into glory. But God is not merely interested in getting you into Heaven; He wants to get Heaven into you!

There are so many wonderful, supernatural demonstrations of power that the Holy Spirit wants to make known in and through your life; so many life-changing experiences the Spirit has in store for you. "Theologically, the basis for seeking renewal is the simple fact that, according to the New Testament, the church is a charismatic community. It exists by God's grace and functions as the gifts of the Spirit manifest themselves in people. The normal Christian experience involves a lively faith in the Spirit as the pivotal reality in human lives."[5] Normality in the Christian life means living a Spirit-directed, Spirit-empowered life which results in Christlikeness and the fulfillment of the unique mission God has for your life.

The quality of your Christian life is dependent upon this discovery of the dynamic ministry of the Holy Spirit. A life of genuine victory over every attack of the enemy can be yours. The Holy Spirit desires to take your love for Jesus and your desire to obey Jesus to a level that is impossible without His power operating at full force in your life. The Spirit will make your life – and your church – a transformative influence in this world. When the Holy Spirit is in full control of a person – or a church – others will know that something different is taking place, something that is not explainable in the natural. You see, your life and ministry are either supernatural or superficial. You are either walking in the power of His Spirit OR you are walking in your own strength. The Spirit of God will make your life "supernaturally natural" and "naturally supernatural" as He fills you with the vitality of Kingdom power!

My Personal Experience

I speak of the ministry of the Holy Spirit from personal experience. I accepted Jesus as my Lord and Savior when I was 17 years old while sitting in a jail cell in Fort Worth, Texas. I came to Christ because of the prayers and witness of three girls in my high school who were so committed to my knowing Jesus that they would not quit praying for me until I was born again. From that moment to this, I have had a burning desire to see others come to the saving knowledge of Jesus Christ.

After being converted, I loved Jesus and wanted everything that He had for me. Sensing God calling me to preach, I quickly entered Bible College to prepare for this call. God immediately began blessing my life and ministry. I knew the hand of God was upon me, and this only increased my hunger for God. I wanted every ounce of God's power to be upon my life.

While traveling full time as a Southern Baptist Evangelist, I met a beautiful Baptist girl from a prominent Baptist family and we were soon married. Great doors of opportunity began opening for me and I started preaching in churches and citywide crusades. Many of the largest Southern Baptist churches in America began inviting me to preach. I preached at every major gathering of my denomination for years, including the Southern Baptist Convention in Indianapolis, Indiana in 1991.

But even with greater blessings and larger opportunities, I knew there was something missing in my life.

I was saved; I loved the Lord Jesus; I loved and read the Bible; I faithfully proclaimed the Gospel; I had the blessings of God on my ministry; and yet I knew in my own heart that something was missing. I read the Book of Acts and saw how the early Christians so powerfully demonstrated the gifts of the Spirit, with healings, words of knowledge and wisdom and other miracles. I wanted that same power and anointing upon my life.

Then I read about speaking and praying in tongues.

Questions for Further Study

1. The Hebrew word for wind in the Old Testament is *ruach*. This word is used to describe the Holy Spirit. It literally means to breathe out through the nose with violence. It is forceful in its impact.

The New Testament Greek word for breath is *pneuma*. This word implies air that is in motion. Look up these scripture references. In your own words, how is the Holy Spirit compared to wind and what are the effects of the wind?

John 3:8
John 20:22
Acts 2:2
Ezekiel 37:9-14

2. The Greek word in the New Testament for fire is *pur*. Fire purifies everything it touches making it glow with light and turning what it burns into its same substance. In the Old Testament we find the Hebrew word *ba-ar* meaning to kindle.

Look up these scripture references. In your own words, how is the Holy Spirit compared to fire and what are the effects of that fire?

Acts 2:3-4
Matthew 3:11-12
1 Thessalonians 5:19
Isaiah 4:4

3. The New Testament word for dove is *peristera*. Its origins are unknown. It literally means dove.

Look up these scriptures associated with the Holy Spirit being likened to a dove. Whom did He descend upon? Other than a possible reference in the Noah account, do you find the Holy Spirit likened as a dove in the Old Testament? Why might that be?

Matthew 3:16
Mark 1:10
Luke 3:22
John 1:32

4. The Old Testament word for power is *koach* meaning
ability. In the New Testament, the word is *dunamis*
which means miraculous power, might, or strength.
Look up these references. In your own words, what is
said about this *dunamis* power? From where does it
come? What are the effects upon the recipient?
Acts 1:8
Luke 4:14
1 Corinthians 2:4
Micah 3:8

"No one ever just picked up the Bible, started reading and then came to the conclusion that God was not doing signs and wonders anymore and that the gifts of the Holy Spirit had passed away. The doctrine of cessationism did not originate from a careful study of the Scriptures. The doctrine of cessationism originated in experience."

Dr Jack Deer in *Surprised by the Power of the Spirit*

CHAPTER TWO

Hungry for More

I was not seeking an experience. I was seeking the power of God. After reading the book of Acts and seeing the miraculous, supernatural power of the Holy Spirit which dominated the men and women in the early church, I wanted that same work and ministry of the Holy Spirit demonstrated through my life.

The Lord Jesus prepared the disciples for this life of power by introducing them to the work of the Holy Spirit. The Son of God entered human history in the Person of Jesus, but never with the idea of remaining or reigning from the earth. He came to establish a kingdom, but always insisted that His kingdom would not be of this world (John 18:36). Rather, He would rule from heaven with the Holy Spirit as His active agent on earth. Jesus' life, death, resurrection and ascension were focused on birthing His followers into the kingdom of God and subsequently baptizing them with the Holy Spirit. Through their redeemed and empowered lives the fallen creation would be restored.

In order to accomplish this Kingly task, Jesus systematically prepared His disciples for a transition from the Old Covenant to the New. He would leave the earth, ascend to the throne of His Father and reign as King of Kings. Simultaneously, King Jesus would pour out the Holy Spirit and His operative power on the earth, baptize His church with the Spirit and direct and empower His church through the work and ministry of the Spirit.

Jesus promised the disciples that the Holy Spirit would be given to the church just days before His crucifixion and resurrection. News that Jesus was about to leave them made the disciples fearful. In light of that fear, Jesus chose He words carefully. "I will ask the Father, and He will give you another helper, that He may be with you forever. I will not leave you as orphans" (John 14:16-18). Initially, the idea of the coming Holy Spirit was not understood or well received by Jesus' disciples.

The disciples were not encouraged. In fact, they were confused, angry and not at all enthused or excited about a new Helper. "What is He saying" (John 16:18), they queried one another. The thought of Jesus being replaced, even by the Holy Spirit, was not what they expected or desired. His strong assurances that He would never leave them "as orphans" (John 14:18) and that "their sorrow would turn to joy" (John 16:7) failed to satisfy them. "But I tell you the truth, it is to your advantage that I go away; for if I do not go away, the Helper will not come to you; but if I go, I will send Him to you" (John 16:7). Only following the resurrection did the teaching of Jesus concerning the coming Holy Spirit become acceptable.

It was essential that Jesus ascend into heaven, receive His Kingdom, take His place on the throne of His father David, and reign as King of Kings and Lord of Lords over everything on the earth, above the earth, and under the earth. In order for His will as King to be accomplished, Jesus would send the Holy Spirit to empower His Church and lead them by faith into the supernatural. Jesus could not complete His work while remaining on the earth and the disciples could not receive all He had for them apart from the reception of a Divine Helper. They needed the Holy Spirit. Jesus told His disciples,

> "I have many more things to say to you, but you cannot bear them now. "But when He, the Spirit of truth, comes, He will guide you into all the truth; for He will not speak on His own initiative, but whatever He hears, He will speak; and He will disclose to you what is to come. He will glorify Me, for He will take of Mine and will disclose it to you" (John 16:12-14).

Jesus' Great Commission mandate could not be carried out without the active ministry of the Holy Spirit. Throughout the Church Age, the Holy Spirit would take the will of King Jesus and communicate it to His Church, filling believers with faith and supernatural power to extend His reign upon the earth, "making disciples of all the nations" (Matt. 28:18-20).

Following His death and resurrection, the apostles gathered in a small room and locked the doors for fear of being killed. Suddenly, Jesus appeared in the room.

Calming their fears, He reassured them of His resurrection by showing them His hands and side. Then once again the topic of His teaching turned to the Holy Spirit. Speaking to them as a group, Jesus said, "Peace be with you; as the Father has sent Me, I will also send you" (John 20:21). His first major act following His victorious resurrection was to regenerate these disciples. "He breathed on them, and said to them, "Receive the Holy Spirit" (John 20:22).

JESUS' GREAT COMMISSION MANDATE COULD NOT BE CARRIED OUT WITHOUT THE ACTIVE MINISTRY OF THE HOLY SPIRIT.

What happened in that moment was miraculous. These men, who had followed Him for three years, believed Him to be the promised Messiah, experienced first-hand His power, had yet to be born again. Now, everything was prepared. Jesus died for the sin of the world and arose triumphant over death. All that was lacking was the power of Holy Spirit, without which, they could not be born again. So, very specifically and individually, Jesus breathed on them and said, "Receive the Holy Spirit." As the Spirit in-dwelled them, they experienced full Christian salvation. At that very moment, the Holy Spirit of God came to live inside of them and quickened their spirits which were dead in trespasses and sins. They came alive! The Spirit of God came to live inside of them and they were born again. Remarkably, the disciples entered the room that Sunday night as faithful Old Testament saints, but they left as New Testament believers.

The Great Reformer, John Calvin, comments on this phenomenon, saying, "Christ breathes into His people, that they may be one with Him."[6] Calvin is describing a fresh and much-needed "baptism" into Christ that the disciples experience as they receive the impartation of the Holy Spirit. From this point on, Christ's original disciples—and all future followers of Christ who receive this purely spiritual baptism (not of water)—would experience a mystical union with Christ through the indwelling presence of the Holy Spirit. The Holy Spirit has not yet come upon them as He will at a later point, but he resides within them. Calvin clearly suggests here that this unique oneness with Christ, for Christ's disciples as with you and I, comes from this initiating experience with the Holy Spirit leading to salvation. This encounter with the Holy Spirit was not the "end-all-be-all" in the disciples' ongoing experience of the ministry of the Holy Spirit but instead an invitation to experience even more of what the Spirit had to offer. What is this "more" that the Spirit has to offer?

The writer of Hebrews hints at the nature of this ongoing gift of the Holy Spirit in the following passage:

> "Therefore leaving the principles of the doctrine of Christ, let us go on unto perfection; not laying again the foundation of repentance from dead works, and of faith toward God, *of the doctrine of baptisms*, and of lay-

ing on of hands, and of resurrection of the dead, and
of eternal judgment" (Heb. 6:1-2; italics added).

I want to focus on the use of the phrase "doctrine of
baptisms" found in this King James Version passage;
some of the more literal translations translate the word
"baptisms" as "washings", but these translations will also
specify in their commentary notes that the original word
here is "baptisms". The use of the plural word "baptisms"
instead of the singular word "baptism" is key since it indicates that there is more than one type of baptism—
more than the typical water baptism that follows a confession of faith. To be clear, as the Apostle Paul says in
Ephesians 4:5, "There is only one baptism...", and that
one baptism is a "baptism" into Christ. But, under the
umbrella of that one "baptism", the Holy Spirit's work of
baptizing us into Christ is progressive and consists of
multiple events such as regeneration, water baptism and
Spirit baptism as we will see is the norm throughout *The
Book of Acts*.

The author of Hebrews discusses these "baptisms" in
the context of explaining what he calls the "elementary
doctrine of Christ". The *Reformation Study Bible*, in its
commentary on the passage, states that all of these essential teachings (or doctrines) can be found in *The Book of
Acts*, which is our record of early church history.[7] What
is interesting to note is that the writer of Hebrews assumes his readers' knowledge of these "baptisms"—which
would likely include both baptisms of water and of the
Holy Spirit—to be fundamental to the Christian faith.[8]
For that reason, he urges readers to pursue more mature

things, spiritually speaking. Could it be that the reason why the American Church remains so deficient in power is because it has not yet grasped all of the "elementary doctrines" of the Christian faith, especially the baptism of the Holy Spirit which typically follows the initial (saving) "baptism" into Christ that the disciples receive? Is the American church like the high school basketball team that tries to perform sophisticated slam dunks without first learning how to pass the ball with accuracy?

Everything is Prepared for You.

If you have not received the saving "baptism" into Christ that the disciples received, you should know that everything is prepared for you to know Jesus as Lord and Savior and be born again. If you don't know Jesus, there is no person, position or possession which can so radically transform and give satisfaction to your life. Psychiatrists can help with a lot of issues, but they can't help with your core problem. Rehab has helped a lot of people to manage addictions, but it can't help with your core problem. There's not a thing in this world that can really set you free. You'll never be fulfilled until you're filled full with Jesus! But when you turn from your sin, trusting in Christ alone as your Savior, asking Him to come into your heart, believing that His death on the cross made atonement for your sin and that by His resurrection He is able to give you a new life, a miracle takes place. Jesus, through the Person of the Holy Spirit, comes into your spirit and begins to live His life in you. This changes everything!

That's what Jesus did in the lives of His disciples. He breathed on them and said, "Receive the Holy Spirit." At that very moment, they were born again. But there was more to follow. They received the first, saving baptism but they needed the second—the baptism of the Holy Spirit.

> *"GO TO JERUSALEM AND WAIT FOR WHAT THE FATHER HAD PROMISED. YOU WILL BE BAPTIZED WITH THE HOLY SPIRIT NOT MANY DAYS FROM NOW"*
> *ACTS 1:4-5*

Now that they were born again, they needed power to serve the Lord Jesus. Their task was to preach the good news of the Kingdom of God to the ends of the earth and as His co-laborers to help Him build the Church. In order to succeed, they would need the power of the Holy Spirit to do supernaturally what they could never do in the natural. So, Jesus told them to wait. Don't go preach yet, instead, "Go to Jerusalem and wait for what the Father had promised. You will be baptized with the Holy Spirit not many days from now" (Acts 1:4-5).

Go Wait!

Finally, Jesus gave His disciples one last promise, "You shall receive power after the Holy Spirit comes upon you and you shall be my witnesses both in Jerusalem, and in

all Judea and Samaria, and even to the ends of the earth"
(Acts 1:8).

For the first eight years of my Christian life, I was a
lot like those newly regenerated disciples. I loved the
Lord Jesus. I was saved. The Holy Spirit lived inside of
me and had sealed me. If I had died, I would have gone
to heaven. But there was a hunger in my soul, a hunger
which only the power of the Holy Spirit could satisfy.

Questions for Further Study

1. "But I tell you the truth, it is to your advantage that I
go away; for if I do not go away, the Helper will not
come to you; but if I go, I will send Him to you" (John
16:7).
The Greek word for Helper is *parakletos* which means an
advocate, intercessor, a consoler, or a comforter.
Look up:
Romans 8:26
Jude 1:20
Galatians 5:22-24

2. What are some ways the Holy Spirit helps us?
Look up:
John 16:13
1 John 5:6
1 Corinthians 2:10

3. In your own words, describe why the Holy Spirit is called the Spirit of Truth.
Look up:
Ezekiel 36:27
Romans 8:11
Acts 6:5

4. Romans 8:11 states that "Christ will give life on account of the Spirit." The Greek word *zoopoieo* used for give life. It means to enliven, quicken, or empower with divine life.
According to our scriptures, what are some ways that the Holy Spirit empowers us?
Look up:
Romans 8:16
Acts 10:19-21
1 Corinthians 12:4-11

5. How does the Spirit communicate to the believer?
Look up:
John 3:4-8
John 6:63
Titus 3:5

6. What is the Holy Spirit's role in salvation?

"The seventh thing that was the secret of why God used D. L. Moody was that, he had a very definite endowment with power from on High, a very clear and definite baptism with the Holy Ghost. Mr. Moody knew he had 'the baptism with the Holy Ghost,' he had no doubt about it. In his early days he was a great hustler, he had a tremendous desire to do something, but he had no real power."

RA Torrey in *Why God Used D. L. Moody*

CHAPTER THREE

The Experience of Pentecost

I searched the Scriptures to find answers regarding the power which I knew was missing in my life. I began to prayerfully read *The Book of Acts.* What did the earliest followers of Christ believe? What did they know that allowed them to walk in such great supernatural power and authority? It quickly became obvious that the answer to these questions was their experience of the baptism of the Holy Spirit. They became radically different people once they were baptized with the Holy Spirit. These first-century Christians entered into a new dimension of kingdom service which required the power of God in order to be effective. The baptism of the Holy Spirit filled them with the power of God. The anointing of the Holy Spirit released the supernatural gifts of the Spirit which began to be dynamically operative in their lives.

I wanted what they had, and I wanted it with all my heart.

What Did They Experience?

Notice the sequence of events described in the narrative of Acts. First, one hundred and twenty men and women were gathered in a single room inside Jerusalem. This happened to be the number of Diaspora Jews stipulated by the Rabbis to form a synagogue in the Graeco Roman world. Included in this group were the apostles along with the core of men and women who had faithfully followed Him during His earthly ministry. The Holy Spirit did not fall upon humanity as a whole. Rather, at Pentecost, Jesus baptized His church with the Spirit. From that point forward, the saving activity of the risen King Jesus upon the earth would be made known exclusively through His church.[9]

Second, this series of supernatural events at Pentecost must be taken as a whole and be understood as occurring simultaneously. The manifestations of the Holy Spirit began with a violent, rushing, heavenly wind which swept in and filled the room (Acts 2:2). This wind was the *pneuma*, the breath of God, signifying the presence of the Holy Spirit. Throughout the Scripture wind or breath is indicative of the Divine presence. Luke's description of the wind of Pentecost calls to mind the experience of the Prophet Ezekiel when the Lord instructed him to preach to the dry bones. The Lord directed Ezekiel,

"Prophesy to the breath, prophesy, son of man, and say to the breath, 'Come from the four winds, O breath, and breathe on these slain, that they come to life.' So I prophesied as He commanded me, and the breath came into them, and they came to life..." (Ezek. 37:9-10).

The bones the Prophet saw represented Israel, the powerless and defeated people of God. The breath was the Holy Spirit whose first task was to bring power to those dead bones so they could rise to be a great victorious army. In the same way, the newly formed Church desperately needed the power of the Holy Spirit to sweep across Her, empowering Her as the army of the Lord, going forth in supernatural power and fulfilling His Great Commission-mandate to bring the nations under His Lordship. This was to be done not only through words of proclamation, but in demonstrations of power, serving notice through signs and wonders that Jesus was no longer in the grave, but was, in fact, alive and well and reigning over all of creation!

Third, the Holy Spirit entered the room and appeared "as tongues of fire resting on each one of them" (Acts 2:3). Exactly how this occurred is not known, but it seems to be flames of fire rising above the head of each individual present, and is most likely tied to the promise of a baptism of the Spirit and fire (Luke 3:16). As is true with wind, the image of fire as a symbol of the presence of God is replete in Scripture. Whatever the exact details, it seems that the Holy Spirit rested upon each of them in a highly visible manifestation of the Spirit's power, individually purifying and preparing them for Kingdom service.

Fourth, each of the one hundred and twenty in the Upper Room "was filled with the Spirit" (Acts 2:4). As much as the tongues of fire were the outer visible manifestation, the fresh outpouring of the Spirit was the inner experience of the Apostles and their fellow disciples.

Finally, each of the followers of Jesus in the Upper Room individually and simultaneously spoke in tongues. "They began to speak in other tongues as the Spirit gave them to speak out" (Acts 2:4). They were baptized by the Holy Spirit and began praising the Lord Jesus in a new language given by the Spirit.

It is critically important to remember who was in the Upper Room: the twelve Apostles and 108 other followers including Mary, the mother of Jesus, Mary Magdalene and other women. Each one of these, including the Virgin Mary, spoke in tongues. The experience was the beginning of the phenomenon of tongues which has continued throughout the history of the church.[10] From that moment forward, the Spirit would place His mark upon the followers of Jesus. They would speak, sing, pray, rejoice and war, by the Spirit, in tongues. New Testament scholar Gordon Fee has noted, "Tongues...was the common, everyday experience of the early churches."[11] The Prophet Isaiah predicted that speaking in tongues would be a sign of the New Covenant, "He will speak to this people through stammering lips and a foreign tongue" (Isa. 28:11).

Speaking in tongues was the sign of the presence of the Holy Spirit and the fulfillment of Isaiah's prophecy. However, the most authenticating aspect of tongue speech at Pentecost was that it occurred in response to the promise of Jesus, "You shall be baptized with the Holy Spirit not many days from now" (Acts 1:5). The experience of the followers of Jesus in the Upper Room at Pentecost was the fulfillment of this promise of Jesus to baptize His people into the power of the Spirit.

At first, it is difficult to understand why the Baptism of the Holy Spirit would include speaking in tongues. Many suggestions have been offered, but for me the simplest explanation is to see the tongues of Pentecost as a reversal of the judgment of God which occurred in the Old Testament. It's the reversal of another miracle that had to do with the tongue and language.

> *...FOR ME THE SIMPLEST EX-*
> *PLANATION IS TO SEE THE*
> *TONGUES OF PENTECOST AS A*
> *REVERSAL OF THE JUDGMENT*
> *OF GOD WHICH OCCURRED IN*
> *THE OLD TESTAMENT.*

After the great flood of Noah, God told the people to multiply and fill the earth. They chose to ignore God and instead build a city with an enormous "tower whose top will reach into heaven" (Gen. 11:4.) Archeologists call the type of building they were planning to construct a ziggurat. Essentially, they were planning to build a mega-church building, saying, "If we can just build it big enough, surely God will come and visit us." It's really not so different from what a lot of churches try to do today. Particularly in the US, the attitude of many congregations seems to be, "If we build it, God (and the people) will come."

So, they began to build their big building and God did come, but He was not pleased with what they were building. Basically, they were trying to approach God on their own terms instead of on His terms. So God judged them at Babel, the place where they were building their ziggurat. At the time, everyone spoke the same language, so God pronounced judgment on their tongues and confused their languages so that they could not understand one another and complete their building project.

The resulting confusion scattered the people to various places in the earth based on common language groupings which eventually gave rise to nationalism, ethnic prejudice and racism. This would ultimately lead to wars and other nationalist or ethnic atrocities that plague the world to this day. Pentecost is God reversing the curse of Babel. Just look at what happened. At Babel, the people came together, all speaking one language; because of disobedience and arrogance, they were scattered into separate nations, speaking different languages. At Pentecost, people who were scattered over these nations were gathered together for this celebration in Jerusalem. The sons of Noah, through whom the entire earth was repopulated following the flood (Gen. 9:19) and scattered in Genesis 11 by the curse of Babel, were regathered at

Pentecost as "devout men, from every nation under heaven" (Acts 2:5). By regathering those who were once scattered, God reversed the curse of Babel. Those who had gathered in Jerusalem for the feast of Pentecost and heard the followers of Jesus speaking in their dialects were amazed.

> "When this sound occurred, the multitude came together and was confused, because everyone heard them speak in his own language. Then they were all amazed and marveled, saying to one another, "Look, are not all these who speak Galileans? And how is it that we hear, each in our own language in which we were born? Parthians and Medes and Elamites, those dwelling in Mesopotamia, Judea and Cappadocia, Pontus and Asia, Phrygia and Pamphylia, Egypt and the parts of Libya adjoining Cyrene, visitors from Rome, both Jews and proselytes, Cretans and Arabs—we hear them speaking in our own tongues the wonderful works of God." So they were all amazed and perplexed, saying to one another, "Whatever could this mean" (Acts 2:7-12).

Unlike Babel, the Pentecostal miracle of tongues did not bring judgment to the peoples of the world, rather it brought Kingdom blessing. Pentecostal tongues are not a curse; they do not result in confusion; they are for the healing of the all the nations. Pentecostal tongues symbolize the breaking down of walls of racism, classism, nationalism and sexism and say to the world, "Something new is happening. God is pouring out His Spirit on all nations!" In the words of Frank Bartleman, reflecting as an eyewitness on the outpouring of the Spirit at the Azusa Street Mission, "The color line was washed away in the blood."[12]

Pentecost also signals the breaking of barriers that have separated the human race since Babel, with the formation of a new humanity in Christ. In other words, Pentecost reverses what happened at Babel. In fact, as Conrad Gempf has shown, something greater happened.

> "In a reversal of the scattering that took place at Babel, the Jewish pilgrim festivals, like Pentecost, brought people from the far corners of the earth to worship God. What is new here is that from now on, people would not need to come back to some central place to worship God-and in the Hebrew tongue. Rather they could go to the far corners of the earth and worship God in their own languages. Moreover, people no longer need to build up to the heavens in search of the significance they lost when they were thrown out of the Garden of Eden. God has now sent his Spirit down to us and lifted our experience to a new level of significance."[13]

The story of the Tower of Babel highlights the stubborn striving of humankind to ascend to the place of the divine, indeed become like the divine. Pentecost, in contrast, showcases the effortless descending of the Divine in the form of the Holy Spirit upon those that He has appointed to receive His priceless baptism. And, since the Holy Spirit is the great initiator in this event, He sets His own agenda—working to remove all of the manmade walls of distinction which we erect between ourselves.

From Pentecost onward, the active presence of the Holy Spirit baptizing, filling and gifting the Church has been normative for the people of God. The record of the New Testament is filled with those who entered into a relationship with Jesus by faith, were born again and subsequently baptized by Jesus into the power of the Holy Spirit, giving evidence by speaking in tongues. At those "power point" moments, the gifts of the Spirit were tangibly visible and audible. Anything less was not Scriptural Christianity. Entering into a relationship with Jesus as Lord and Savior was never stale or formal; rather the gifts of the Spirit were always present. Spirit baptism was always supernatural and the supernatural was always demonstrated by acts of prophetic speech, in particular, speaking with other tongues. This pattern is normative in the Book of Acts.

As I read the biographies of great Christians, I noticed that many of my heroes, particularly those used mightily in evangelism, testified to receiving what they deemed an empowering baptism of the Holy Spirit subsequent to their salvation. Men like John Wesley, Charles Finney, D. L. Moody, R. A. Torrey, Billy Sunday and even Billy Graham spoke of a life- altering encounter with the Spirit which changed forever the course of their ministries. I began to seek after this same kind of empowerment, often crying out to God, "Fill me or kill me." I was desperate for God's power!

Questions for Further Study

1. Look up Acts 2:4
How many were filled with the Spirit?
What did they begin to do?
Who gave the utterance?

2. Look up Acts 1:8
What did Jesus say would happen when they received power from on high?
With this in mind, what do you think Paul meant when he said that "tongues were a sign for unbelievers?" (1 Cor. 14:22)
Having read about the Holy Spirit's role in breaking down cultural barriers, how do you think tongues would aid in that process?

"The epochal significance of Pentecost raises the whole course of salvation history to a new plane...In one sense, therefore, Pentecost can never be repeated- the new age is here, and cannot be ushered in again. But, in another sense...the experience of Pentecost can and must be repeated in the experience of all who would become Christians."

New Testament Scholar James Dunn in *Baptism in the Holy Spirit: A Re-examination of the New Testament Teaching on the Gift of the Holy Spirit in Relation to Pentecostalism Today*

CHAPTER FOUR

What Does This Mean?

There was no crowd of thousands expectantly waiting outside the Upper Room for the coming of the Holy Spirit. Indeed, what happened in the Upper Room did not take place for the benefit of a crowd, but for the empowerment of the disciples of Jesus. It was only after the events of the Upper Room that a crowd gathered. "When this sound occurred, the crowd came together..." (Acts 2:6).

What sound occurred? Some contend it was the sound of the rushing wind that caused the crowd to come together, but the rushing wind was confined to the whole house where they were sitting. The supernatural sound which the crowd heard was the one hundred and twenty men and women corporately praying, singing, and praising God in tongues. The followers of Jesus apparently had been speaking and worshipping in tongues in the Upper Room for an extended period of time.

The timeline is significant. First the events in the Upper Room took place. After time passed, the crowd gathered, and the disciples were still speaking and praying in tongues. Only then does the crowd overhear what was taking place *inside* the Upper Room.

What happened at Pentecost, as the Apostle Paul would later explain, was a sign to the lost (1 Cor. 14:22).

> "Now there were Jews living in Jerusalem, devout men from every nation under heaven. And when this sound occurred, the crowds came together and were bewildered because each one of them was hearing them speak in his own language. They were amazed and astonished, saying, "Why, are not all these who are speaking Galileans? "And how is it that we each hear them in our own language to which we were born?" (Acts 2:5-8).[14]

Many in the crowd were positively amazed, while others were openly skeptical. "Are these people drunk?" Immediately, the disciples understood what was happening and its significance. Based upon what Jesus told them following His resurrection, they instantly believed this phenomenon was the work of the Holy Spirit and the will of heaven.

Pentecost and the New Covenant

The Apostle Peter quickly decided to address the crowd. In doing so, he preached the first Christian sermon declaring the Messiahship of Jesus and declaring that the outpouring of the Holy Spirit had initiated the

New Covenant. "Men of Judea and all you who live in Jerusalem, let this be known to you and give heed to my words. These men are not drunk, as you suppose, for it is only the third hour of the day; but this is what was spoken of through the prophet Joel..." (Acts 2:14-16).

Pentecost was not strange. It was not to be avoided and was not simply for the moment. Rather, Peter declared, "this is what was spoken through the prophet Joel". Pentecost fulfilled the prophetic promises of Joel and forever established that the era of the Messianic Kingdom of God's great Son would be the age of the Spirit.

> "It shall be in the last days,' God says, `That I will pour forth of My Spirit on all mankind; and your sons and your daughters shall prophesy, and your young men shall see visions, and your old men shall dream dreams; even on My bondslaves, both men and women, I will in those days pour forth of My Spirit and they shall prophesy" (Acts 2:17-18).

The Prophet Joel did not forecast the end of the world or the Second Coming of Christ; rather, he prophesied that in the last days the Lord Jesus would baptize His Church with the Holy Spirit. The Apostle Peter reached back to Joel and interpreted his poetic and prophetic language to describe the dual activities of King Jesus throughout the New Covenant era. From His throne in heaven, ruling as King of kings, the anointed Messiah, Jesus, would baptize His Church with the Holy Spirit and pour judgment out on His enemies. The initial baptism of His Church occurred at Pentecost.

This was the celebratory launch of the Church of Jesus Christ. From this day on and to the end of the age, Pentecost, with its attendant Charismatic gifts, could not be ignored or pushed aside. Pentecost was the remarkably radical and singularly unique event that gave birth to a very specific Christianity, and as a result, "Everyone who calls on the name of the Lord will be saved" (Acts 2:21).

At its birth, the church was global. Though it would take time for the church to fully comprehend and embrace, because of the outpouring of the Holy Spirit, the Gospel of the Kingdom was immediately open to everyone with no restrictions. The Pentecostal phenomena gave an impetus to a community of believers who were destined to break through social, racial, and religious barriers with a message of light and life for all mankind.

Peter continued focusing on the supernatural ministry of the Lord Jesus that came as the result of this baptism of the Holy Spirit. "Men of Israel, listen to these words: Jesus the Nazarene, a man attested to you by God with miracles and wonders and signs which God performed through Him in your midst, just as you yourselves know..." (Acts 2:22).

The entire earthly ministry of Jesus was one of miracles, signs and wonders by the power of the Holy Spirit. Peter insisted these miracles were not the result of Jesus' exercise of His divine attributes; rather, Jesus displayed miraculous signs of the Kingdom as a human filled with the Spirit of God. They were signs that God performed through Him. Obviously, Peter was referring back to the man Jesus being baptized in the Holy Spirit (John 1:32).

As a man, Jesus walked day by day in radical dependence upon God the Spirit, prayed, and spoke by the power of the Spirit. In portraying Jesus as constantly dependent upon the Spirit, the Gospels were not challenging or questioning his deity or divine Sonship. Rather, as eternal Son the theandric person already was truly God, while as a man, Jesus was truly human, bone of his bone, flesh of our flesh, seed of Abraham, whose humanity was continually replenished by the Spirit (Luke 4:14; Heb. 2:14-17). He did not walk or speak by his own independent human power, but by the power of the Spirit. Every gift requisite to the Son's mission was provided by the Spirit.[15]

Jesus' reliance upon the Spirit to fulfill the will and call of God His Father upon His life is a model for His disciples. It is in observing Jesus that His disciples receive a visual of what the Spirit-led life looks like. Likewise, it is in studying the lives and exploits of the apostles that we gain a picture of the Spirit-empowered life. Their pioneering lives, along with that of Jesus, paint the canvass of our imaginations, providing us with the resource of faith-inspiring vision to challenge our preconceived notions of what is possible in and by the Spirit.

A few years ago, I found myself receiving such vision to believe God for the miraculous in my life and ministry. I pastored for over twenty-two years and when God spoke to me about resigning my church and going back on the road as an Evangelist, one of my main concerns was how to provide for the financial needs of my family. Our oldest daughter, Sarah, was in her third year of college. Our oldest son, Dillon, was a junior in High School with Josh and Madi not far behind. I was out on my daily walk and, quite honestly, was having a frank conversation with the Lord about my concerns. I distinctly heard the Lord say to me, "Look down on the ground." I remember that it was a cool, windy day in the month of February. I slowed a bit and looked down, not knowing what I was looking for and for the next 10 minutes I continued to walk and look and after seeing absolutely nothing, I began to think that perhaps I was coming a bit unhinged.

I remember thinking, "I've finally lost it. I'm hearing voices!" Then the Lord spoke again. "Look down on the ground," He said, in a voice louder than audible. There, dancing in the wind, caught in a blade of grass, was a folded up bill. The Lord said, "Pick it up." I excitedly reached down, expecting to pick up a hundred dollar bill and instead retrieved a crisply folded "George Washington!" I remember thinking, "Man this is weird. I really heard from God. This is most certainly no coincidence." (Incidentally, I spent the next several years on my daily walk looking for more money and finding nothing. The incident was repeated 4 years later, however. Another miraculous story I must save for another time.)

But I also remember thinking, "Lord, why isn't this a $100 bill. I could really use a $100 right now!" Here's what the Lord said. "Son, what if it was a $100? What if it was $1000? You need hundreds of thousands of dollars for what I've called you to do around the world. This is a SIGN. A sign is always something small which points to something larger than itself." He reminded me of the several signs throughout the Bible: a rainbow, a young woman becoming pregnant, an unknown language. All of these signs pointed to greater realities. All of them are indicative of a promise appropriated by faith. Then the Lord promised, "Son, if you will trust me, obey me and follow me into this season of ministry, letting go of the financial security of being a pastor, neither your family nor your ministry will ever suffer lack." This happened over 5 years ago and God has been faithful to His Word. I relearned that day the importance of hearing the voice of God speaking through His Spirit.

...ANOTHER ASPECT OF THE BAPTISM OF THE HOLY SPIRIT IN THE BOOK OF ACTS WAS SUPERNATURAL POWER.

Along with God-given vision, another aspect of the baptism of the Holy Spirit in *The Book of Acts* was supernatural power. It was true for Jesus; it would be true for His church. As Peter would later explain to the members of Cornelius' household,

> "You know of Jesus of Nazareth, how God anointed Him with the Holy Spirit and with power, and how He went about doing good, and healing all who were oppressed by the devil, for God was with Him" (Acts 10:38).

Peter declared that this supernatural power and authority was the direct result of Christ's victory over death.

> "This Man, delivered over by the predetermined plan and foreknowledge of God, you nailed to a cross by the hands of godless men and put Him to death. "But God raised Him up again, putting an end to the agony of death, since it was impossible for Him to be held in its power" (Acts 2:22-24).

The Son of God, incarnated in the person of Jesus of Nazareth, could not be held by the power of death. The Apostle Peter stood on the balcony of the Upper Room and introduced his audience to a new interpretation of the prophecy of Joel and then to the promises to David of the enthronement of his greater Son, the Lord Jesus Christ.

> "Brethren, I may confidently say to you regarding the patriarch David that he both died and was buried, and his tomb is with us to this day. And so, because he was a prophet and knew that God had sworn to him with an oath to seat one of his descendants upon his throne, he looked ahead and spoke of the resurrection of the Christ, that He was neither abandoned to Hades, nor did his flesh suffer decay" (Acts 2:29-31).

The Apostle declared in the clearest possible terms that the power of sin and death had been defeated by the awesome reality of Jesus' resurrection. Christ had won! As a result of His great victory, all of the promises God made to David concerning the kingdom were now being fulfilled. David prophetically looked ahead and spoke of the resurrection of the Christ. The prophetic promise given to David had not been postponed to the end of the age. Jesus had ascended back to His Father and was seated upon the throne of His father David in heaven and was now ruling as the Messianic King. The future had broken into the present through the ministry of Jesus!

Peter's Pentecost sermon ended with two climatic declarations: "Therefore having been exalted to the right hand of God, and having received from the Father the promise of the Holy Spirit, He has poured forth this which you both see and hear" (Acts 2:33). The outpouring of the Spirit on the celebration of the Feast of Pentecost was the beginning, the inauguration of a new age, the age of the Spirit. It was the moment in which King Jesus, the Messiah, the resurrected man, the Son of God, demonstrated that His Church would forever be a supernatural people operating in the power, gifts and the anointing of the Holy Spirit. "Therefore let all the house of Israel know for certain that God has made Him both Lord and Christ--this Jesus whom you crucified" (Acts 2:36).

What the followers of Jesus experienced in the Upper Room and what the crowd overheard was the enthroned Jesus acting upon His kingly prerogative to pour out the Holy Spirit upon His people. This outpouring was the heavenly declaration to the earth with outward, visible, audible demonstrations that Jesus was both Lord and Christ!

The crowd was stunned! Pierced to the heart with conviction, they cried out to Peter, "What shall we do" (Acts 2:37)! Peter responded with what became the essential steps of Christian initiation.

> "Repent, and each of you be baptized in the name of Jesus Christ for the forgiveness of your sins; and you will receive the gift of the Holy Spirit. For the promise is for you and your children and for all who are far off, as many as the Lord our God will call to Himself" (Acts 2:38-39).

"REPENT."

"BE BAPTIZED."

"YOU WILL RECEIVE THE HOLY SPIRIT."

The pattern of initiation was forever established. "Repent." Christian repentance was not a mere cataloging of sins, but a change of mind about and a turning from sin to receive Jesus as Lord and Savior. "Be baptized." Publicly identify yourself, through water baptism, with the death, burial and resurrection of Jesus. "You will receive the Holy Spirit!" No doubt Peter has in mind both the initiatory work of the Spirit at conversion as well as the subsequent and vocational empowerment of the believer. Understood correctly, the Baptism of the Holy Spirit is the expected experience for each Christian.

There was no hesitation for Peter. His assurance was based upon what he knew was the essential expectation:

following the salvation experience, each new Christian would be baptized with the Holy Spirit. The Apostle Peter assured those who responded to his message that "they could experience what the apostles had experienced," which was what the Father had promised (Acts 1:4). Therefore, from Pentecost forward, each individual who receives Jesus as Lord and Savior is to then be baptized with the Holy Spirit, and that baptism was to always include the open demonstration of the gifts of the Spirit, and that most definitely included speaking in tongues.[16] Since the Lord Jesus chose to empower His Church in this way, no one has the permission or authority to change the pattern and attempt to build the church or live the Christian life without the power of the Holy Spirit.

The Church Requires This Power

There is no lack of churches today. The last thing needed is more churches that are going to be as powerless as every other church. Without the power of God filling our lives and churches, this will be the result: more of the same. A powerless church is just another country club with a steeple on top. Francis Schaeffer writes:

> The central problem of our age is not liberalism or modernism, nor the old Roman Catholicism or the new Roman Catholicism, nor the threat of communism, nor even the threat of rationalism and the monolithic consensus which surrounds us [nor, I would add today, postmodernism or materialistic consumerism or visceral sensualism or whatever]. All

these are dangerous but not the primary threat. The real problem is this: the church of the Lord Jesus Christ, individually or corporately, tending to do the Lord's work in the power of the flesh rather than of the Spirit. The central problem is always in the midst of the people of God, not in the circumstances surrounding them.[17]

If we compare the early church with the American church, one of the clear differences is an absence of power in the church today. This power shortage is a direct result of our relying on our own resources to get things done. The Holy Spirit, who took the center stage at Pentecost, has sadly been relegated to the back pew at best in many of our churches.

This is the last thing the Lord Jesus wants for His Church. Jesus wants to fill us with the Holy Spirit, not merely for the purpose of having an experience, but in order that we may share the good news of Jesus Christ with power and literally change our world. This was the impact of the Acts church. Within a generation, this Spirit-empowered church shook the Roman Empire to its very core. They did this without the benefit of technology, Bible colleges and seminaries, television or radio ministries, Christian bookstores or Facebook memes! What was their secret? They had received a mighty baptism of the power of the Holy Spirit!

The early Christians were bold witnesses of the life, death and resurrection of Jesus. They testified with such irrefutable conviction and power that they were often martyred. I meet many so-called Spirit-filled Christians today who seldom if ever witness to anyone. They seem to be ashamed of Jesus outside the walls of their church buildings. You would have a hard time convincing these early believers that you're a Spirit-filled Christian if you never tell anybody about Jesus! The promise in Acts 1:8 was that the power of God would come on us, enabling us to be witnesses to the ends of the earth. The Apostles turned the world upside down because they were filled with the Holy Spirit. We're called to do the same – and to do it, we need the same empowering baptism of the Holy Spirit. This Great Commission ministry is not to be carried out in "word only." It is to be carried out in the "demonstration and power of the Holy Spirit" (1 Cor. 2:4). Such Holy Spirit power would soon come to characterize my ministry as a Southern Baptist Evangelist. It would come at a great cost.

Questions for Further Study

1. Look up Acts 2:1-13
Can you map out the timeline described in this chapter? What sound did the crowd hear?

2. Look up Acts 2:22
The word miracle means powerful deeds, deeds showing (physical) power, marvelous works.
Wonders are defined as a miraculous *wonder*, done to elicit *a reaction from onlookers*; an extraordinary event with its supernatural *effect* left on all who are witnesses.

Signs (typically miraculous), are given specially to confirm, corroborate or authenticate.

According to Acts 2:22, why were these miracles, signs, and wonders given?

3. Look up Psalm 103:1-5.

David lists 5 benefits of the kingdom, what are they?

How does this relate with Acts 10:38 when it says that Jesus went about healing all those that were oppressed by the devil?

4. Look up Matthew 28:18

This scripture says that Jesus has given us His authority. According to our study questions above, what does this given authority mean for us? How long will Jesus be with us?

"The Holy Spirit has long been the Cinderella of the Trinity. The other two sisters may have gone to the theological ball; the Holy Spirit got left behind every time, but not now. The rise of the Charismatic Movement within virtually every mainstream church has ensured that the Holy Spirit figures prominently on the theological agenda. A new experience of the reality and power of the Spirit has had a major impact upon the theological discussion of the person and work of the Holy Spirit."

Alister McGrath in *Christian Theology: An Introduction*

CHAPTER FIVE

The Original Pattern

The outpouring of the Holy Spirit did not end at Pentecost. Rather, the baptism of the Holy Spirit became an essential aspect of Christianity, the event of empowerment for the Church of Jesus Christ. The Holy Spirit entered the life of each man and woman who genuinely repented and fully committed his or her life to Jesus Christ as Lord and Savior. The presence of the Holy Spirit in an individual's life was the guarantee of their salvation and relationship with God (1 John 4:13). If a person had not received the Holy Spirit, they had not experienced the salvation of Jesus, and were not part of His Church (John 14:17; Gal. 4:6; 1 John 3:24). But the early Church recognized there was another experience with the Holy Spirit which was absolutely indispensable. This is clearly understood throughout *The Book of Acts.*

The Baptism of New Jewish Christians

There are six additional Pentecost-type outpourings of the Spirit found throughout the book of Acts. For example, days after the events described in Acts 2, another group of Christians experienced a similar outpouring. Between Acts 2 and Acts 4, some 5,000 persons received Jesus as Lord and Savior (Acts 4:4). Following their salvation, they were all together when suddenly, the Spirit moved upon this new group and they were baptized with the Holy Spirit. "When they had prayed, the place where they had gathered together was shaken, and they were all filled with the Holy Spirit and began to speak the word of God with boldness" (Acts 4:31).

The Baptism at Samaria

The same pattern is seen at Samaria. Following the scattering of the church in Jerusalem brought on by violent persecution; Philip entered Samaria, the cosmopolitan city of Sebaste, and preached the Gospel of the Kingdom, declaring Jesus to be the Christ, the long awaited Messiah. This was a bold and courageous mission for the deacon-evangelist. The Samaritans were like ordinary Jews in some ways, but totally unique in others. They were strict monotheists and worshiped Yahweh as did the Jews, but their religion was not mainstream Judaism. Samaritans were a racially mixed society consisting of both Jewish and pagan ancestry who differed from the Jews on the location of the Temple (John 4:20), the line of priests, and the exact books and content of the Torah. In some respects, they were more legalistic than Jews regarding the Mosaic Law; especially the Sabbath regulations.

Because of their unorthodox adherence to Judaism and their mixed ancestry, the Samaritans were despised by the Jews. Rather than be contaminated by passing through Samaritan territory, Jews superstitiously journeying from Judea to Galilee or vice versa would cross over the river Jordan, by-pass Samaria and cross over the river again as they neared their destination. The Samaritans also harbored a deep-seated antipathy toward the Jews (Luke 9:52-53).

There were religious tensions between the Samaritans and the orthodox Jews, economic differences between the urban and peasant economies, and radical distinctions between the cosmopolitan cities of the Samaritans. Samaritans served in the army of Herod, which meant that they were sometimes used against the Jews of Judea or Galilee. This did little to increase sympathy between the two peoples. To make matters worse, when the Jewish War broke out in 65-66 AD, the inhabitants of Sebaste saw their city razed to the ground by the Jews as they fought the Roman Army. So the sight of a Christian deacon-evangelist from Jerusalem into Sebaste would not have been well-received. But that did not deter the Spirit-empowered Philip!

When the deacon demonstrated the veracity of his message by the power of the Holy Spirit with signs, healings, and authority over unclean spirits, the people of the city quickly responded with great rejoicing (Acts 8:5-8). As a result of their response to the Gospel, Philip did as he should have done, he baptized them. "When they believed Philip preaching the good news about the kingdom of God and the name of Jesus Christ, they were being baptized, men and women alike" (Acts 8:12).

Those who were baptized did not receive the baptism of the Holy Spirit. They believed and were baptized in water, but they had yet to receive the baptism of the Holy Spirit. Philip quickly sent word to the Church in Jerusalem and requested the Church to send apostolic assistance. The Apostles Peter and John were dispatched from Jerusalem to join Philip in Samaria. "Now when the apostles in Jerusalem heard that Samaria had received the word of God, they sent them Peter and John, who came down and prayed for them that they might receive the Holy Spirit. For He had not yet fallen upon any of them; they had simply been baptized in name of the Lord Jesus. Then they began laying their hands on them, and they were receiving the Holy Spirit" (Acts 8:14-17).

It is apparent from these events that the Samaritan Christians accepted the salvation of Jesus, experienced water baptism and yet had not received the baptism of the Holy Spirit and its attendant power.

Once the Apostles Peter and John arrived to assist Philip, they quickly remedied the situation. "Peter and John… prayed for them that they might receive the Holy Spirit… Then they began laying their hands on them, and they were receiving the Holy Spirit" (Acts 8:14-17).

When the Samaritans were baptized with the Holy Spirit, something supernatural and verifying happened. The Spirit entered and brought His gifts. Based on the other descriptions of outpourings of the Holy Spirit in the Book of Acts (Acts 2, 10, 19), the evidence indicates that each of the Samaritans spoke in tongues. But without a doubt, something very obvious and clearly demonstrative instantly occurred. Before there were no visible gifts of the Spirit, then Peter and John laid hands on them and the gifts were present, which meant the Spirit was present. When the prophetic gifts were demonstrated by these new Samaritan Christians, there was no longer any doubt that they had been powerfully baptized with the Holy Spirit.

Whatever the exact events, it was so impressive that Simon Magus wanted to buy the power to replicate the phenomenon. "When Simon saw that the Spirit was bestowed through the laying on of the apostles' hands, he offered them money, saying, "Give this authority to me as well, so that everyone on whom I lay my hands may receive the Holy Spirit" (Acts 8:18-19).

Peter was furious, openly rebuked Simon and declared, "May your silver perish with you, because you thought you could obtain the gift of God with money! You have no part or portion in this matter, for your heart is not right before God" (Acts 8:20-21).

When Peter and John saw the faith of the new Samaritan Christians, they knew exactly what was needed. They preached, prayed, and laid their hands on these new believers. And it worked! The Samaritan converts were baptized with the Holy Spirit. When the Spirit was poured out, the supernatural manifestation of His presence was obvious to all, for they spoke in tongues. The Samaritans moved out of their sins, beyond the natural, and into the supernatural power of Jesus, the reigning King.

The Baptism of Gentiles

The experience of the Roman Centurion Cornelius (Acts 10) in the city of Caesarea was a series of radical supernatural manifestations which climaxed with each person present being born again, baptized with the Spirit and speaking in tongues. As a Centurion and commander of a Roman cohort, Cornelius was a ranking officer in the Roman Army, commanding nearly 500 men. His rank allowed him to have his family with him in the garrison. What set Cornelius apart was not simply his military courage and ability, but the great love and devotion he and his household shared for God. They prayed continually and helped many of the Jewish people over whom he held political and military control. One day, probably while praying, he had a vision of the angel of God who came to him and said, "'Cornelius!' And fixing his gaze on him and being much alarmed, he said, 'What is it, Lord?' And he said to him, 'Your prayers and alms have ascended as a memorial before God. Now dispatch some men to Joppa and send for a man named Simon, who is also called Peter; he is staying with a tanner named Simon, whose house is by the sea'" (Acts 10:3-6).

Cornelius obeyed immediately, and ordered three of his soldiers, one of whom was also devoted to God, to go to Joppa and find Peter. The Apostle was in prayer awaiting the evening meal when he fell into a trance and God opened to him His desire to reach the Gentiles.

"Peter saw the sky opened up, and an object like a great sheet coming down, lowered by four corners to the ground, and there were in it all kinds of four-footed animals and crawling creatures of the earth and birds of the air. A voice came to him, "Get up, Peter, kill and eat!" But Peter said, "By no means, Lord, for I have never eaten anything unholy and unclean." Again a voice came to him a second time, "What God has cleansed, no longer consider unholy." This happened three times, and immediately the object was taken up into the sky" (Acts 10:11-16).

These orders overwhelmed Peter's Jewish mind and lifelong prejudice. It took a direct order from the Holy Spirit to override Peter's religious bigotry and allow him to be used as the instrument of the work of the Spirit. The Holy Spirit spoke to Peter saying, "Behold, three men are looking for you. Get up, go downstairs and accompany them without misgivings, for I have sent them Myself" (Acts 10:19-20).

Like Cornelius, the Apostle Peter obeyed. His obedience was a great miracle. As Peter would later share with Cornelius, for a Jew to enter the world of a Gentile without being forced was unthinkable. But Peter had received direction from the Holy Spirit Himself. So, he went downstairs and presented himself to Cornelius' soldiers,

"I am the one you are looking for; what is the reason for which you have come?" They said, "Cornelius, a centurion, a righteous and God-fearing man well spoken of by the entire nation of the Jews, was divinely

directed by a holy angel to send for you to come to his
house and hear a message from you" (Acts 10:21-22).

After hosting these Gentile soldiers in his home for
the night, they departed Joppa the next morning for the
trip up the coast of the Mediterranean to Caesarea. Ar-
riving at Caesarea they went directly to the house of
Cornelius. The Centurion, his family and many of his
friends who shared his deep desire to know God were
anxiously awaiting Peter. "When Peter entered, Cornelius met him, and fell at his feet and worshiped him.
But Peter raised him up, saying, "Stand up; I too am just a
man" (Acts 10:24-26).

Peter had walked into a hotbed of spiritual anticipa-
tion. There was great excitement among those who had
gathered at Cornelius' house. Their hearts were hungry;
their expectation was great. After Peter got Cornelius up
from his knees and they shared the common visions they
had experienced, the Apostle was thoroughly convinced
this mission to Caesarea was a divine appointment. Peter promptly turned the topic to Jesus—His power over
evil, His awesome ability to heal and forgive sins, and
most importantly, Jesus' great victory over death at the
cross.

> "You know of Jesus of Nazareth, how God anointed
> Him with the Holy Spirit and with power, and how
> He went about doing good and healing all who were
> oppressed by the devil, for God was with Him. We
> are witnesses of all the things He did both in the land
> of the Jews and in Jerusalem. They also put Him to
> death by hanging Him on a cross. God raised Him up

on the third day and granted that He become visible, not to all the people, but to witnesses who were chosen beforehand by God, that is, to us who ate and drank with Him after He arose from the dead... through His name everyone who believes in Him receives forgiveness of sins" (Acts 10:38-43).

Resisting the reservations of some of those who had accompanied him, the Big Fisherman faithfully preached the Gospel of the Kingdom. As Peter did what he could do, the Holy Spirit did what only He could do! "While Peter was still speaking these words, the Holy Spirit fell upon all those who were listening to the message" (Acts 10:44).

This supernatural move of the Holy Spirit absolutely shocked and amazed Peter and the company of Jewish Christians who were present. In their minds, Gentiles coming into the salvation of the Jewish Messiah could never occur. Yet, Gentiles were not only being saved, they were being baptized in the Spirit! The question must be asked, how did Peter and those with him know that the Holy Spirit had baptized them? The answer is simple: something supernatural and conspicuous manifested, and they all heard it. Just like Pentecost and Samaria, the evidence of Spirit baptism was recognizable to all those who were present. "All the circumcised believers who came with Peter were amazed, because the gift of the Holy Spirit had been poured out on the Gentiles also... for they were hearing them speaking with tongues and exalting God" (Acts 10:45-46).

Each individual in Cornelius' house simultaneously spoke with tongues! This was the visible and audible sign, the mark of the Holy Spirit placed upon the Gentile believers. Instantly, the Apostle Peter and the Jewish Christians understood the ramifications. Gentiles had entered the Kingdom, were brothers and sisters in the Church of Jesus Christ and were baptized in the power of the Holy Spirit.

EACH INDIVIDUAL IN CORNELIUS' HOUSE SIMULTANEOUSLY SPOKE WITH TONGUES!

That night in Caesarea, Christian initiation was turned on its head. Before the Gentiles were baptized in water or Peter finished preaching or the Apostle had laid his hand upon them or they prayed the sinner's prayer, they were born again. It was as though the Holy Spirit was reminding all of those with Peter and subsequently Christians throughout the Church Age that salvation was His prerogative. As Jesus said to Nicodemus, "The wind blows where it wishes." Peter spoke through his shock and declared, "Surely no one can refuse the water for these to be baptized who have received the Holy Spirit just as we did, can he?" (Acts 10:47).

The silent, resounding answer was, "NO!" No one could refuse, no argument could be raised because salvation was being unmistakably experienced by the Gentiles and each of them was clearly baptized with the Holy Spirit just as the Church had experienced at Pentecost.

This was not a private prayer moment standing in the back of the room. Each one of the new Christians at Cornelius' house simultaneously spoke in tongues! Peter ordered them baptized in water.

The Baptism of Paul

It is difficult to imagine a more unlikely convert to Christianity than Saul. Born in Tarsus of Cilicia around 5 AD to affluent parents who had obtained Roman citizenship by their wealth, Saul was an educated radical Jewish zealot who described himself as a descendent of Abraham of the tribe of Benjamin, a Hebrew of Hebrews, Pharisee and a son of Pharisees (Acts 23:6) who lived according to the strictest sect of Judaism (Acts 26:5), and one who was blameless according to the Law. This young Jewish extremist, educated under Gamaliel with strict adherence to the Law of the fathers, was so deeply opposed to Christianity that he saw as his life work the persecution and eradication of what he believed to be a false Messianic sect. On his own initiative, Saul sought and received authority from the High Priest to arrest Christians and bring them to Jerusalem for punishment. Despite Roman rule, the Sanhedrin claimed the same authority over Jews throughout the Diaspora that they exercised at Jerusalem.

> "Now Saul, still breathing threats and murder against the disciples of the Lord, went to the high priest, and asked for letters from him to the synagogues at Damascus, so that if he found any belonging to the Way,

both men and women, he might bring them bound to Jerusalem" (Acts 9:1-2).

Saul terrorized the Church and they feared his rampage against them. While on the road to Damascus to continue his campaign against the followers of Jesus, something supernatural occurred. Jesus confronted Saul. The Lord would not tolerate this zealot's destruction of His young Church. The Lord's confrontation carried with it the ultimate possibility, but not the certainty, of Saul's conversion, and fully allowed the exercise of Saul's will.

Added to the unlikelihood of Saul's conversion is the unlikelihood of the place near his conversion: Damascus. Damascus, in some ways, was the communal equivalent of Saul—a hotbed of Jewish, religiously-inspired violence, especially against their Roman oppressors. "The Jews in Damascus were very numerous; and there were peculiar circumstances in the political condition of Damascus which may have given facilities to conspiracies or deeds of violence conducted by the Jews."[18] Yet, God does in the unlikeliest person and near the unlikeliest place what only God can do—bring an unrepentant, hatred-filled sinner to his knees.

Questions surround Saul's conversion, especially concerning the process. Was Saul instantly saved on the road to Damascus, or did his salvation take place at the end of a three day period? The answer lies in the timeline of the actions of Jesus, a Christian named Ananias and Saul.

First, as Saul continued to Damascus, around noon, "...suddenly a light from heaven flashed around him; and he fell to the ground and heard a voice saying to him, "Saul, Saul, why are you persecuting Me" (Acts 9:3-4)? The entire scene quickly became one of complete bewilderment. The Jewish companions of Saul were speechless, and fell to the ground as dead (Acts 26:14). Each heard the voice, but saw nothing. Stunned, dazed, disoriented, bewildered and probably lying flat on his back, Saul cried out in his confusion, "Who are You, Lord" (Acts 9:5)?

Saul certainly knew of the messianic claims of Jesus and the supposed salvation He had promised to His followers. So it is certainly within the realm of probability that Saul immediately knew who was confronting him. Saul's cry was an expression of holy fear and awe that may have contained a confession of salvation.

Secondly, Jesus understood Saul's cry as salvific, responding, "I am Jesus whom you are persecuting..." This was Jesus the compassionate Savior speaking to a repentant enemy of His Church. The Lord Jesus added, "...get up and enter the city, and it will be told you what you must do" (Acts 9:6).

The men with Saul quickly moved to help him up from the ground. When he stood, he was blind so they took him by the hand and led him into Damascus. Saul entered Damascus full of questions and remained in a state of spiritual shock for three days not eating or drinking.

Third, the Lord spoke to Ananias, a Jewish Christian at Damascus, in a vision and said to him, "Get up and go to the street called Straight, and inquire at the house of Judas for a man from Tarsus named Saul, for he is praying..."

The dramatic events Saul experienced during the three days between his encounter on the road to Damascus and his baptism were pivotal. In all likelihood, Saul was instantly changed and immediately embraced Jesus as his new Lord and Messiah. Saul had literally been stopped in his tracks, physically and spiritually knocked to the ground. The Lord would not allow him to go forward the same. Throughout the three days of fasting and prayer Saul was coming to grips with who Jesus was and the content and demands of His Gospel and Kingdom. No doubt he thought of the martyr Stephen and his sermon chronicling the promises of Yahweh to send a Deliverer to save His people. It all began to make sense. How would Saul respond? What would he believe? And, what would this mean for his life? Would he pay the price the Lord was demanding of him? Saul was in the throes of conviction, and had been told by Jesus that a man named Ananias would, "...come in and lay his hands on him, so that he might regain his sight" (Acts 9:11-12).

Naturally, Ananias was hesitant because of Saul's reputation as a hater and destroyer of the Church, but the Lord assured him, "Go, for he is a chosen instrument of Mine, to bear My name before the Gentiles and kings and the sons of Israel..." (Acts 9:15). If Saul chose, he would receive both his salvation and commission at the hands of Ananias.

Fourth, Ananias obeyed, knowing that specific steps must be accomplished in Saul's life to complete his commitment to Jesus and assure his salvation. When Ananias entered the house where Saul was staying, Saul was blind, gaunt from lack of nourishment and remained in a state of confusion. Ananias graciously ministered to Saul. "Brother Saul, the Lord Jesus, who appeared to you on the road by which you were coming, has sent me so that you may regain your sight and be filled with the Holy Spirit" (Acts 9:17; emphasis added).

Most likely, Ananias was overly precise, desiring to clearly present the Gospel of the Kingdom to Saul and assure his understanding. Then, knowing Saul had truly accepted Jesus as Lord and Savior, Ananias laid his hands on Saul's head. This was a powerful prayer of healing to end the blindness. When Ananias prayed, the Holy Spirit moved supernaturally to answer Saul's prayers. He was immediately healed from his blindness and baptized with the Holy Spirit. "...immediately there fell from his eyes something like scales, and he regained his sight, and he got up and was baptized..." (Acts 9:18).

Saul's conversion must be viewed as one experience, lasting from the encounter with Jesus on the road to Damascus and climaxing with the ministry of Ananias. But, as was true in the stories of Pentecost, Samaria and Cornelius, the baptism of the Holy Spirit was subsequent to Saul's salvation.

There is not a specific reference indicating that Saul spoke in tongues as a sign of Spirit baptism, though considering the pattern in *The Book of Acts* and his testimony in the Corinthian letters regarding his prayer life it would be an anomaly if he did not experience tongues at that time. What is undeniable is the depth of the experience of Saul. He was radically changed. This event was so dramatic that he would carry it throughout his ministry as the Apostle Paul and insist upon its duplication by all who would come into the salvation of Jesus. We know from his own testimony that speaking, praying, and singing in tongues were all very important to the him (Acts 19; 1Cor. 14:18), and that being the case, more than likely, speaking in tongues was part of the experience as he was baptized with the Spirit. One thing for certain, that day in the house of Judas the tanner at the hands of the powerful man of God Ananias, something supernatural happened to Saul. Saul's salvation was complete when he called on Jesus as Lord, then, and only then, could he receive the baptism with the Holy Spirit evidenced by speaking in tongues.

The Baptism in Ephesus

Twenty-years following Pentecost, the Apostle Paul arrived at Ephesus. He was greeted by a dozen men, presumably Jewish, who to his surprise were disciples of John the Baptist, but possessed at least some knowledge of "the way." They were living in a kind of "half-way house" between Judaism and Jesus. In Acts 19, the Apostle Paul immediately began an inquiry to help ascertain their relationship to the Lord Jesus. The Apostle's targeted question indicated the essentiality of the Holy Spirit in the experience of the Christian. Paul did not ask if they knew Jesus, if they had been saved, if they had prayed the sinner's prayer, if they had repented of their sins, if they had been baptized, or even if they understood the gospel. The emphasis was not on a specific prayer, but on an experience. Were these men Christians? If they had been baptized with the Holy Spirit, then certainly they had been saved. Every question would become clear with a single question regarding the Holy Spirit. The Apostle asked, "Did you receive the Holy Spirit when you believed?" (Acts 19:2).

This was the question, the normal inquiry that came from Paul's own experience. Certainly Paul would not have asked an irrelevant question in an attempt to find truth. Their response clearly indicated their spiritual condition. "No, we have not even heard whether there is a Holy Spirit" (Acts 19:2).

Paul immediately questioned the validity of their baptism. As far as Paul was concerned, if they were not aware of the ministry of the Holy Spirit, their water baptism was illegitimate and their salvation was nonexistent! He responded, "'Into what then were you baptized?' And they said, 'Into John's baptism'" (Acts 19:3).

They had been baptized with John's baptism, though not necessarily by the Baptist himself. These men had only heard of Jesus within the context of that community. Recognizing where they were in their understanding of the person and work of Christ, the Apostle took them methodically, step by step through the claims of Jesus and the requirements of salvation. Paul taught, "John baptized with the baptism of repentance, telling the people to believe in Him who was coming after him, that is, in Jesus" (Acts 19:4).

Once they heard the Gospel of the Kingdom they gladly received Jesus as Lord and Savior. Following their salvation, Paul baptized them in water identifying them with the name of the Lord Jesus. Most likely as each individual came up from the waters of baptism, the Apostle Paul, "...laid his hands upon them, the Holy Spirit came on them, and they began speaking with tongues and prophesying" (Acts 19:5).

Something happened! In a demonstrable event twenty-five years following Pentecost, each of these new Christians was baptized with the Holy Spirit spoke in tongues and prophesied. This is the pattern. With the coming of the Spirit at Ephesus, Luke's chronology of the outpouring of the Holy Spirit in the *Acts of the Apostles* was complete. He had historically established the requirements and expectations of the Church Age regarding the baptism of the Holy Spirit.

From that point forward, it was expected that each individual who received Jesus as Lord and Savior was to be baptized with the Holy Spirit, resulting in power to bear witness to the realty of Christ's resurrection. For those believers, whether at Jerusalem, Samaria, Caesarea, Damascus or Ephesus, the miraculous gifts of tongues and prophecy gave evidence to this outpouring.

I would soon experience my own similar and life-altering "Pentecost."

Questions for Further Study

1. Read Ephesians 2:11-22
The Greek word for dividing wall is *phragmos*. It literally means fence, or that which keeps two from coming together.
What we read about in chapter 5 are different groups that had obstacles to overcome in order to receive salvation and the baptism of the Holy Spirit.
.

2. Jewish Christians: Read Acts 4:23-37
Why were the Jewish Christians praying for boldness?
What kind of dividing wall or obstacle was standing in their way of being united together in Christ?
After they were filled with the Spirit, what happened?
According to Acts 4:32, what had happened?

3. Samarians: Acts 8:4-25
What caused the newly converted Christians to leave Jerusalem and preach to other people groups?
What was the dividing wall that needed to be brought down in Samaria?
Acts 8:6 states that the crowds in Samaria were in one accord as they listened to Philip preach. What caused their interest?
What was their response in Acts 8:8?

4. The Roman Centurion

When Acts 10:1 says that Cornelius was a devout man who feared God, it is a reference to a specific group of people who were not considered Jewish, but had a respect for the God of the Jews and His ways.

What was the dividing wall that needed to be brought down in order for Cornelius to be saved? Was it on the part of Cornelius, Peter, or possibly both?

What happened to both men that got their attention?

Acts 10:44-48 shows us the results of the obedience of both men. What happened? What was the evidence and why was that important?

5. The Baptism of Paul

What dividing walls needed to be brought down in order for Paul to receive salvation and the Holy Spirit?

What happened when Ananias prayed for Saul in Acts 9:17-19?

Where did God send his chosen vessel after he was filled with the Spirit? (Acts 9:20-22).

What was the one of the results of Saul's conversion in Acts 9:31?

6. The Baptism in Ephesus

What was the dividing wall that needed to be brought down in Acts 19:1-6?

What happened when Paul laid his hands on these twelve men and prayed?

How did these twelve men help Paul?

"I do not recollect any Scripture wherein we are taught that miracles were to be confined within the limits of the apostolic age or the Cyprian age, or of any period of time, longer or shorter, even till the restitution of all things. I was once fully convinced of what I had once suspected...that the grand reason why the miraculous gifts were so soon withdrawn was not only that faith and holiness were well nigh lost, but that dry, formal orthodox men began even then to ridicule whatever gifts they had not for themselves, and to decry them all as either madness or imposture."

Rev. John Wesley, Founder of Methodism

CHAPTER SIX

You Need the Baptism of the Holy Spirit

There are two distinct works the Holy Spirit wants to accomplish in your life. The first occurs when you accepted Jesus as Lord and Savior. At that moment, the Spirit brought the life of God into your dead spirit, and you were born again. Paul the Apostle wrote, "You were dead in trespasses and sin... but God made us alive" (Eph. 2:5). Simultaneously, the Spirit baptized you into the Body of Christ (I Cor. 12:13). This is Christian salvation. Once you are saved, the Holy Spirit begins to work in your life. He begins the process of sanctification and maturity, making you more and more like Jesus from the inside out. Paul refers to this as the "fruit" of the Spirit produced in our lives. This process, the building of

Christ-like character, can be described as the "within" work of the Holy Spirit.

There is also a second work of the Holy Spirit which is subsequent to salvation. This second work is described by Luke beginning in Acts 2. Quoting the Prophet Joel, Peter says that the "last days" will be characterized by the Holy Spirit being "poured out" upon all of the people of God. This "upon" work of the Spirit creates a prophetic community, whose purpose is to powerfully bear witness to the reality of the Kingdom of God come to earth. This is the fulfillment of Moses' desire that the Spirit would rest upon all God's people and that they would all prophesy (Num. 11:29). Every believer has experienced the "within" work. Every believer needs to experience the "upon" work!

"We are nothing less than a community of end time prophets called and empowered to bear bold witness for Jesus."[19] You may not think of yourself as a prophet or prophetess, but a prophet is simply someone who speaks boldly on behalf of God under the guidance and inspiration of the Holy Spirit. When you receive the baptism of the Holy Spirit like the Christians in *Acts*, you receive the authority to speak with courage. You also receive the power to demonstrate the reality of the Kingdom through signs and wonders.

Sarah's Story

One Saturday morning, after making several hospital visits, I pulled into the parking lot of our local Starbucks. My intention was to spend a few hours looking over my notes for the Sunday's message while enjoying my favorite Italian Roast coffee prepared in a French coffee press. All of this was interrupted by a devastating phone call. A voice barely audible due to some strange background noise asked, "Is this Pastor Scott Camp?" I answered in the affirmative wondering what on earth could be making the loud, pulsating noises on the caller's end of the conversation. Then came the news, "My name is John Smith and I'm calling from a Care-flight helicopter. Your daughter Sarah has been hit by a car on the street in front of your home. We are flying her to Children's Hospital in Dallas. Sir, you need to get there as quickly as you can."

My heart surged. This is every dad's worse nightmare. Sarah was 9 at the time, our first born and a daddy's girl through and through. She captured my heart from the first moment I laid eyes on her. God has used her to soften the tough kid who still had so many childhood wounds.

Two things happened simultaneously in that moment. One, I put on my hazards and broke every speed limit and ran every stop sign and red light from Plano to Dallas. Secondly, I immediately began to pray. I prayed with both my understanding and my spirit. I prayed that God would spare the life of my beautiful little girl. I prayed in tongues, sobbing with unutterable groaning and trusting the Spirit to tell the Father that which I found unable to communicate with my natural faculties.

Over the next few hours the word got out to our church family that Sarah had been in a terrible accident.

One dear friend took a bucket of soap and water and washed the pool of Sarah's blood from the busy road in front of our home. She said she didn't want Gina to have to see her daughter's blood or have anyone run over the spot in the road where the speeding pizza delivery car had driven her head-first into the asphalt road. I'll never forget the kindness of Morgan Taylor on that dark day.

Several dozen church family members filled the waiting rooms of the hospital and began crying out to God, standing in the gap interceding for Sarah's life to be spared and for God to bring miraculous healing to her injured head. From the first the doctors informed us that due to the severe head trauma which she had suffered, skin grafts would need to be taken from her thighs and extensive plastic surgery would be needed. Hundreds of stitches had closed the wound in her scalp but there was no skin to sew together the tear inflicted in her forehead and hairline. Of course we consented to anything necessary and rejoiced that in spite of the accident, no permanent brain damage had been detected and infection had miraculously not set in to the exposed cranium. This was a tremendous relief to all of us and we celebrated with thanksgiving the good report.

My step-mother, Sarah's "Nana," had been in the medical field for quite some time and knew every doctor at Children's Hospital on a first-name basis. She asked to be present in the operating room as the doctor began preparations to do the painful skin grafts necessary to close Sarah's head wound.

Change the scene for a moment. At the exact same time, a missionary friend of ours was having a prayer meeting and Bible study in a home in a neighboring city. His testimony is that as he began to pray God gave him a vision of Sarah. Please keep in mind that he knew nothing of the accident. He said he saw her face and God spoke to him to pray for Sarah's head. Something was wrong with Sarah Camp's head. (I'm weeping as I am writing this and reliving the greatness of our Father and His providential care for us!) Our missionary friend, Dub Lewis, said that he rather casually mentioned this to the folks gathered for prayer and Bible study. They agreed together that Father would touch and heal whatever the problem was with little Sarah's head.

That was it. They went on with their study.

Back in the OR, Nana overheard the surgeon say to a nurse, "There's really no skin here to work with but I hate to do this painful procedure on this young girl. I'm going to try one more time to close this wound." And that is when it happened!!! My medically trained and scientifically minded step-mom said that like Jesus' miracle of multiplying fishes and loaves, God began to powerfully multiply skin cells in our Sarah's head! The doctor said, "I don't know where this skin is coming from but every time I need to make a stitch there it is." No skin grafts. No brain injury. No infection.

Today, my Sarah is a graduate of Criswell Bible College and is investing in the next generation by using her teaching gift to change the lives of children. She says her three inch scar is a reminder of God's power and Lordship over her life!!! I believe in the power of God!

The "Upon" Work of the Spirit

When the Holy Spirit is poured out, He releases the sign gifts of the Kingdom already resident within the Christian. One of these powerful gifts is speaking in tongues. So, does that mean that you need to speak in tongues? Yes! This is one of many gifts which the Holy Spirit wants to manifest through you. You may say, "I don't want to speak in tongues." Well...then you probably never will. But, think about it, don't you want *everything* God has for you? This would be like a groom asking if he must kiss the bride! Do you really want to turn away *any* gift that God has for you?

There are many people who acknowledge that speaking in tongues is legitimate – after all, it's obviously described in the Bible – but they insist that speaking in tongues is not for everyone or that not everyone will speak in tongues. Those who want to limit the use of tongues often cite 1 Corinthians 12:30, "Do all have gifts of healings? Do all speak with tongues? Do all interpret?" Clearly, this passage is referring to an "ecclesia" gift which, when used within the context of the gathered church, should be interpreted. At this point in corporate worship, the Spirit releases another gift, the ability to interpret the message given in tongues, so that the entire church is edified, comforted and exhorted. This is qualitatively the same as prophecy.[20] But tongues as an initial physical evidence of Spirit baptism is for all believers.

This aspect of the tongues gift is for worship, intercession and personal edification. I reiterate—it is for all believers.

Every believer in *The Book of Acts* spoke in tongues. The Bible specifically states that they all began to speak in languages which they had never learned (Acts 2). It became a sign that the walls of separation which have divided humankind since the Fall had been torn down and that the reign of God was now filling the earth. The age to come has broken into the present evil age.

> *IT BECAME A SIGN THAT THE WALLS OF SEPARATION WHICH HAVE DIVIDED HUMANKIND SINCE THE FALL HAD BEEN TORN DOWN...*

The Lord Jesus wants *you* to speak in tongues. He wants *you* to prophesy. He wants *you* to heal the sick. He wants *you* to cast out demons. And these miraculous signs are not just to take place within the four walls of the church building. The power of God is to be demonstrated out in the real world of the workplace, at your school and in your neighborhood. People are desperate to see and experience the life of Christ. The lost world is not impressed with church people, no matter the denominational tag we may wear. The truth is, they have seen our shallow, pathetic excuse for a Christian life. They have seen us fight and squabble, split churches, take each other to court, market the Gospel and scandalize the name of Jesus.

What they want to see and experience is the life of Jesus flowing in and through His Spirit-filled people. The sad truth is that the average believer doesn't have enough power in their life to blow the fuzz off a peanut! All the while, there's a world outside the four walls of the church building which desperately needs a touch of God. The Lord Jesus wants to pour His Spirit out upon you, so that you can go and impact the world in which you live! I once heard Billy Graham say that 95% of all Evangelicals will not win another person to Jesus within the course of their lifetime. Something is obviously wrong!

The Feast of Pentecost was a celebration of the giving of the Law at Sinai. Moses went up into the mountain and was enveloped in a cloud of God's glory. When he descended the mount, he brought God's law, engraved by the very finger of God upon stone tablets. This giving of the Law constituted (along with the priesthood, temple and sacrificial system) the religion of Israel. The rest of the Old Testament is the story of Israel's failure to keep the Covenant established at Mount Sinai. The Jews were very religious, but their forms and rituals seldom touched and transformed human hearts. But God promised through His prophets that the day would come when a New Covenant would be established and God would put His Spirit within His people and write His law upon their hearts (Jer. 31:33; Ezek. 36:27).

This promise was fulfilled on the Day of Pentecost. Just as Moses ascended to heaven, Jesus ascended to heaven; just as Moses descended with the law of God, Jesus, in the Person of the Holy Spirit, descended from heaven and actualized the promised New Covenant by writing God's law on the hearts of His New Israel and coming to empower them to keep the Law of Christ, given in His famous "Sermon on the Mount." New Covenant people are people of the Spirit. They are not "religious" in the sense of performing empty rituals. In the words of U2's Bono, "Religion is what happens when the Spirit leaves the room." He's exactly right! People of the Spirit carry the infectious joy of Pentecost. They celebrate the law of God written on their hearts, which can be summarized in the teaching of Jesus that we should love God and love our fellow image-bearers as we love ourselves. This new level of love is the essence of the Spirit-filled life.

This is true as much in the New Testament as in the Old. God's way of empowering us to live rightfully before Him has always included reliance on and the indwelling of the Holy Spirit (despite the inability of Old Testament believers to really understand this truth and flesh it out). The law and the Holy Spirit work hand-in-hand to produce the desired result of a loving life in the heart and mind of the indwelled believer.

> The law and its witness to righteousness will only find fulfillment through the in dwelling of the Spirit. The law cannot create singleness of heart in devotion to God, new hope in the midst of despair, give new life, or raise up the dead. The law as a letter or a norm cannot fulfill righteousness. The law and its powerful

witness to God live from the Spirit and depend on the gift of the Spirit in the Old Testament. The promise of righteousness in the context of living by the law essentially involves even more fundamentally the promise of new life in the Spirit.[21]

Fulfilling the law involves walking in step with the Holy Spirit and obeying the dictates of His promptings, which are in accordance with Scripture. The law is void of any power in and of itself to bring human hearts into alignment with God's will and purposes; only the Holy Spirit can do that through the indwelling of wholly surrendered believers.

Pentecost was also an annual time when Israel celebrated the ingathering of their crops. The people of God would dance, rejoice, feast and drink, all in thanksgiving to God for the blessing of harvest. The Pentecostal outpouring of the Spirit was also a time of great harvest. As Peter stood to explain the phenomenal demonstrations of God's power in light of the death, resurrection, ascension and exaltation of Jesus the Christ, 3,000 people were convicted, converted and confirmed via water baptism. This ingathering resulted in great joy which shook Jerusalem and began to spread like a prairie fire, eventually reaching the capital city of the Empire.

If you're born again and on your way to heaven, that's awesome, but that isn't all there is to the Christian life. God wants to pour His Spirit out on you so that you can walk in the same Spirit and love that Jesus walked in and reach out to the lost, the marginalized, the hurting, just like He did. In fact, "the gift of God always results in mission" and thus God wants to speak through you by the Person of the Holy Spirit.[22] And yes, God does still speak today. Don't let anyone tell you He doesn't. God did not write the Bible and afterward become mute. You can't read through the Book of Acts without constantly seeing the Holy Spirit speaking to His people and giving them specific directions.

Why would God include these stories in the Bible if He did not intend such experiences to be the normal experience of all His people? The Spirit wants to speak to you, like He recently spoke to me at a grocery store, saying, "Do you see that lady over there? I want you to go right over there and this is what I want you to tell her. 'I know that this might sound strange to you, but I love Jesus with all my heart and I love you and the Lord wants me to tell you...'"

I experience this on a regular basis. I've seen people break down and begin weeping as Spirit-filled believers begin to tell them about circumstances in their lives which no one could have known in the natural. I've seen them come under deep conviction. I've seen people led to Jesus this way. One of the biggest problems we have in the church is that we seem to think that we need to bring people to a church service or to a crusade in order to get them saved. I've preached at hundreds of churches and held evangelistic crusades for years and I've seen tens of thousands come to Christ in this way. I'm 100 percent in favor of mass evangelism, but God wants to fill all of His people with His Holy Spirit – not just the Billy Grahams of the world – so that we can all go tell the world about Jesus and know the joy of leading a lost person to the Savior. The early church was a Spirit-baptized fellowship where everyone went everywhere, every day, by every means available, powerfully proclaiming and demonstrating the Good News of the Kingdom. This is the ongoing evidence of the Spirit-filled life!

It is important that all we do in the name and power of the Spirit also be done in and through the love of the Spirit for the hurting and lost around us. Pentecostal scholar Frank Macchia says that without love, Spirit baptism would be, "little more than raw energy without substance or direction, feeding little more than an emotional release....Love is God's supreme gift, for it transcends all emotion, conceptuality, action, only to inspire all three....There is nothing beyond love."[23] The believer whose life and actions point most powerfully to the baptism of the Spirit exhibits both the fruit and the gifts of the Spirit. Love is the essential fruit and motivation for the missional life of the Spirit-baptized person and church.

Questions for Further Study

1. Look up 1 Corinthians 12:28-31
Many have been taught that 1 Corinthians 12:30 is proof that all will not speak in tongues. But if we put this in its proper context, Paul is referring to what setting? Personal or the corporate assembly?

2. Look up 1 Corinthians 14:12-17

1 Corinthians 14:12 talks about the use of spiritual gifts and the edification of the church. Throughout 1 Corinthians, where the "gift of tongues" is present in the corporate assembly, what must also be present?

Why is this so?

What are the guidelines for tongues during the assembly as a corporate gift in operation?

How do we reconcile this with the fact that all that received the baptism of the Holy Spirit, spoke in tongues?

If we look at tongues in the larger context of the New Testament, we find that tongues were the normative Christian experience. The guidelines in 1 Corinthians are for the corporate worship setting.

3. Jude:20-21 says, *"But you, dear friends, by building yourselves up in your most holy faith and praying in the Holy Spirit, keep yourselves in God's love as you wait for the mercy of our Lord Jesus Christ to bring you to eternal life."*

According to this passage, praying in the Spirit does what for our personal lives?

Much of the teaching in today's church on tongues adds greatly to dividing us theologically. However, we know that the Holy Spirit breaks down dividing walls.

What are some of the dividing walls that would be brought down if every believer knew that tongues was for them and for today?

"Criswell Dean fired over Speaking in Tongues"

Dallas Morning News, February 1, 2006

CHAPTER SEVEN

Crossing Over

As a young Southern Baptist evangelist, God blessed our ministry with thousands of converts. Suddenly I was receiving invitations to preach in some of the largest churches in America. During this time, I met one of my heroes in evangelism, a former Southern Baptist, who shared with me his charismatic experience. I found his story to be quite unsettling and yet my heart was captivated and I knew that it was this type of experience for which I longed.

Each time I preached, many came to receive Jesus as their personal Lord and Savior. Simultaneously, I was filled with an inner hunger for a deeper supernatural relationship with the Lord Jesus, and a greater power in ministry. Many nights after I preached, I was genuinely joyful and thankful to the Lord for allowing me to be used as His instrument, yet I was also aware of an unrest, a lack of satisfaction, a knowing there had to be more in my experience of the Lord Jesus and His ministry than I was touching.

Later that year, I preached several nights in Oklahoma City at a great Southern Baptist church pastored by a wonderful man who was graduated from New Orleans Baptist Seminary with a Ph.D. Eventually, he relocated to Nashville and became a member of the Executive Committee of the Southern Baptist Convention.

One night a leader of a local Satanist group came to observe and mock the message of salvation in Jesus. Rather than interrupting the work of the Holy Spirit, this young man was convicted of his sin and surrendered his life to Jesus. The next night he was back and brought with him row after row of the wildest looking kids I'd ever seen in my life. They were all dressed in black from head to toe. As I preached the gospel, the Holy Spirit did a powerful work. When I gave the invitation to receive Jesus over 150 young people came to commit their lives to the Lord and receive His salvation including all of those who had been involved in Satanism and the occult. They were saved and delivered from demons that night!

After the service, the ringleader who had been saved the night before told me that although he had accepted Jesus as Lord and Savior he was still hearing voices. He said that the voices told him to kill his family and then to commit suicide. I warned him that Satan wanted to destroy his life. We prayed for him and immediately he was delivered from demonic torment. What a night!

Following that remarkable service, I said to the pastor, "Let's get your staff and my team and go into your office. Let's pray and thank God for what He did to-night." He agreed, so we all crammed into his small office. From the start our prayers were intense as we praised the Lord and genuinely thanked Him for allowing us to be used of Him in such a remarkable way. One by one, various individuals prayed out loud as all of us joined in supporting them. I was thrilled to be there, to have experienced the night of great victory, to have seen Satan so thoroughly defeated and Jesus so wonderfully accepted and praised.

That's when it happened!!

Spontaneously, without any predisposition, I began to pray aloud in tongues!! It was so unexpected, it literally frightened me. For a moment, I wondered if the demons who were cast out of those kids had entered me. After all, I had gone to a Bible college which taught that if a person spoke in tongues, it was probably the devil.

Don't Be Afraid of the HOLY SPIRIT

At that moment, the Holy Spirit very gently said to me, "Son, this is the sign of my power! It is the sign that the release of power you've longed for, what you've prayed for, looked for and hungered for has been poured out in your life. This is the experience you have read about in the book of Acts, and thirsted for in your life.

This is the sign that I am doing a new thing in your life and ministry."

Let me be totally honest with you. I left the prayer meeting that night freaked out! But if you think I was freaked out, you should have seen my wife. Speaking in tongues was strange to me, but it was totally out of bounds for Gina!

I had been a Southern Baptist youth pastor and then a Southern Baptist evangelist for a few years, but she was practically Southern Baptist royalty. On the way home that night my little Baptist wife, to whom I had been married only a couple of years, asked me, "What on earth were you doing?" "Were you ... speaking in tongues?" "Do you do that?" "We're Baptists!" "We don't do that!" "My parents don't do that!"

Remember, I grew up in a bar and got saved in a jail cell, but she had been in the Baptist church from the time she was in her momma's womb. Her dad was a Southern Baptist pastor; her brother was a Southern Baptist pastor; her mother went to a Baptist seminary; her brother went to a Baptist seminary; her sister went to a Baptist seminary and married a Southern Baptist pastor. She gave her life to Jesus at a Southern Baptist tent revival where her brother was leading Southern Baptist worship and stepped down from the Southern Baptist platform to lead his little 7-year-old Southern Baptist sister to Southern Baptist Jesus! She had loved Christ and had lived for Him all of her life as a Southern Baptist. Now, her Southern Baptist husband was speaking in tongues!

All through the night I felt like I was wrapped in a warm blanket of the love of God. The next day, I met with the pastor who had been with me in the prayer meeting the night before. We had a very interesting conversation. I sheepishly said, "Pastor, something very unusual happened while we were praying last night."

"Oh yes, I heard," he replied. When I asked him what he thought about it, he very calmly asked, "Do you believe it was of God." I looked directly in his eyes, and said, "Yes, yes sir, I do."

He smiled and said, "Scott, a lot of us have had very unusual experiences with the Holy Spirit. We just don't talk about it. You have a great ministry as an evangelist among Southern Baptists, but if you tell anyone about this experience or begin to preach about it, you'll be ruined. My advice to you is to keep it very private." And that is what I did for years.

From that point forward, things have been different for me. I could not deny what had happened to me, nor did I want to. My prayer life has exploded into whole new realms of supernatural faith. I love to pray, and every day I pray in tongues. I have greater confidence because of the experience. I preach with a more powerful anointing than I had before. Every time I preach, people are saved, healed, delivered from demonic strongholds and freed from destructive habits. I live and minister at a new level of power and authority which I did not have before. Something wonderful and powerful happened that night in that small office.

Pentecostal scholar Frank Macchia says,

> "In the meantime, humans experience Spirit baptism as the Spirit is manifested to their experience in moments of ecstasy and self-giving. Ecstasy is not only an emotion but there is also a sense that one can transcend oneself in embracing God and the neighbor. Spirit baptism in the New Testament thus gives rise

to a profoundly personal- though not individualistic-
experience."[24]

In essence, he is saying that the experience of personal
Pentecost is one that is both inward and outward in its
scope; the Holy Spirit does a profound work within the
believer, but that internal stirring and transformation
also directly results in the impact of people and, thus, the
world around you. Both an awe-inspiring sense of oneness with God and a gentle compulsion to lovingly reach
out to others with spiritual need accompany baptism in
the Spirit. This two-fold blessing is what I was experiencing, and it was blowing my mind!

Although I felt and experienced the change, it was
years later before I found the courage to openly talk
about my experience with the Holy Spirit. And the pastor was right. When I finally did begin to share what I
had experienced, it cost me a lot.

I have found that the Jesus you preach and the Jesus
you expect is the Jesus that will show up. I preached a
saving Jesus right from the start of my ministry, and as a
result, thousands of people were saved. Praise God for
that! I still preach a saving Jesus and I am seeing more
people come to Christ than ever before. But as I began to
preach a Jesus who also heals – because that's the Jesus
the gospel writers tell us about, the One they preached
about in *The Book of Acts* – and people began to experience healing. I began to preach a Jesus who delivers
from demonic strongholds and I've seen people set free
that couldn't be set free by drug rehabs or psychotherapy.
They were touched and set free by the power of Jesus! I

began to preach a Jesus who blesses His people when they're obedient to Him. In other words, I began to preach the full gospel: Jesus as Savior, Healer, Deliverer and Baptizer in the Spirit.

> *EXPERIENCING THE FULLNESS OF THE SPIRIT HAS ALSO DELIVERED ME FROM DEEP-SEATED FEELINGS OF RACIAL SUPERIORITY AND SEXIST ATTITUDES TOWARD WOMEN.*

Experiencing the fullness of the Spirit has also delivered *me* from deep-seated feelings of racial superiority and sexist attitudes toward women. My early Christian life was spent in the middle-class, white and male-dominated world of Fundamentalist Evangelicalism. I don't think I was conscious of these privileged attitudes in all those years. Certainly I would have never owned these feelings. But looking back, I can see clearly that they formed a major part of my theology and worldview. After being baptized in the Holy Spirit, God began to set me free from these fleshly feelings of superiority. I began to see the power of God demonstrated through my sisters and brothers of color. I learned that the dominant characteristic of the New Age of the Spirit in Acts 2 is that the Spirit will be poured out on everyone. The Spirit of prophecy invites and involves both sons and daughters! "Privileges based upon gender or age or social standing...end when the Spirit is poured out."[25] The democratization of the Spirit is one of the telling signs of the Kingdom of God "already" present!

Building Bridges, Not Walls

Years ago I was the Pastor of a large, wealthy suburban church. The ten million dollar campus sat on 60 acres of well situated property in the fastest growing city in the southern end of the county. We were experiencing rapid growth and many of the members were catching a vision for reaching everyone moving into this once sleepy little enclave of white America.

So I was shocked when I walked into a meeting of the "Property and Space Committee" and was greeted with disappointment over the decision by the city council to approve plans for multifamily apartment housing to be built on land contiguous with that of the church. I was overjoyed at this prospect. I remember clearly expressing my heart in words like, "Wonderful" and "Praise God!" As the conversation ensued, I shared my vision of pouring a sidewalk from the back of the apartment complex to the front of the church building and throwing a "Welcome to the Neighborhood" party for the new families, complete with bounce houses, a cook out, clowns, and a Gospel Magician for the kids. I was excited about the potential of reaching hundreds of new folks for Jesus.

These church leaders were not so thrilled, however. The Chairman expressed his concern that such a complex would no doubt soon fill up with low income, mostly minority, single mothers. "Nothing will devalue our property as quickly as these kinds of people living in that kind of housing," was his reply to my plan. "As a matter of fact," he declared, "we are not going to build a sidewalk, we are going to build a wall."

It was at this point that I heard the Spirit clearly and gently speak, "Son, you are released from this assignment. I'm not interested in dividing people. I'm interested in bringing them together."

This deeper relationship with the Spirit has also broadened my understanding of the nature of Scripture. As a new believer, I was encouraged to read, study, meditate upon and memorize the Bible. I fell in love with the Bible! I loved the stories of the Old Testament characters and could relate to their struggles to obey the Lord and defeat their enemies. I loved the doctrines of the Bible, particularly those found in the writings of the Apostle Paul. I enrolled at a very conservative Bible College which was at the forefront of a "battle" against perceived encroaching liberalism within the Southern Baptist Convention. It was there that my simple devotional reading and study of the Bible was transformed into theological reflection, including the study of the original languages in which the Bible was written. I loved church history, philosophy and systematic theology. I still enjoy these disciplines. But, subtly, my simple child-like devotion and passion to hear the voice of God speak to me through my quiet time was transformed into dissecting the Biblical text for fascinating information about authorship, original setting and theological content. Slowly but surely, the technical study of the Bible and theology had replaced my love and desire to hear the voice of the

Spirit through scripture. The Bible and particularly Western theology had become an "idol" in my life!

Sometimes, I feel that many of my cessationist friends (those who believe that certain gifts of the Spirit, including tongues and prophecy have ceased) worship God the Father, God the Son and God the Holy Bible. They fear that if we desire, accept and embrace the powerful revelatory gifts of the Spirit, that this will somehow diminish the authority of Scripture in our personal lives and in the life of the Church. One cessationist summed up the experience of speaking in tongues which is so prominent in the Charismatic/Pentecostal movement in the following way:

> By contrast (to the NT gift), the modern Charismatic version consists of non-miraculous, nonsensical gibberish that cannot be translated. It is a learned behavior that does not correspond to any form of human language. Rather than being a tool to edify the church, contemporary Charismatics use the fabrication as a private "prayer language" for the purpose of self-gratification. Though they justify their practice because it makes them feel closer to God, there is no biblical warrant for such unintelligible babble. It is a false spiritual high with no sanctifying value. The fact that modern glossolalia parallels pagan religious rites should serve as a dire warning of the spiritual dangers that can be introduced by this unbiblical practice.[26]

Many cessationists see glossolalia, speaking in tongues, as a modern invention of half-crazed, hyper-emotional and quasi-heretical Christians who seek to experience something that just is not available for us to experience today. They ignore the reality that a vibrant minority of Christians have always practiced the charismatic gifts throughout Christianity's 2000+-year history and that speaking in tongues has borne tremendous, verifiable spiritual fruit in the lives of millions of contemporary believers. But, perhaps more importantly, it is precisely by following the pattern of Spirit baptism in the Bible, and particularly in *The Book of Acts*, that continuationists (those who believe that the revelatory gifts are for today) arrived at their conclusions concerning the Holy Spirit's desire to do today what He did in the early church. Thus, it is cessationists (not continuationists) who created a paradigm-shifting way of relating to the Holy Spirit which goes against the witness of the Spirit's normative activity as revealed in the Bible!

When we examine the formation of the Bible, it is clear that the Holy Spirit inspired its authors. He superintended their work, using their backgrounds and knowledge and often even helped them choose the exact words to convey their thoughts. He preserved their writings and guided the Church through history to canonize certain texts which we know as our Christian Scripture. But the Spirit has never been limited to the text of the Bible in revealing His mind and will to His people. He also speaks through dreams, visions, historical events and through supernatural spiritual gifts including speaking in tongues, interpretation of tongues, prophecy, words of wisdom and words of knowledge. How do we know that the Spirit operates in these ways? Simply because the Bible tells us so!

The Bible contains the record of God's revelatory acts in time and space. It tells the story of God's desire to communicate to His image-bearers in less than perfect historical conditions. This is obviously the case in the aftermath of the fall of man. God continued His relational pursuit of His fallen, broken people in a fallen, broken world. This meant that He would have to speak to humans in ways and through means which they could understand. The cultural contexts in which Scripture was written often reflect the deep brokenness of the post-Edenic world. This is true in both the Old and New Testaments. For example, Paul's instruction for women in the city of Ephesus not to teach men and his injunction for slaves to submit to their masters, are conditioned by the first century culture in which Paul lived. "In fact, Paul demonstrates (throughout the rest of First Timothy) that he is not in favor of restricting the role of women in the church on the basis of gender."[27]

The Holy Spirit was thrusting the Church, through the ministry of the Apostle, beyond the provincial boundaries of Judea and into the belly of the Greco-Roman world. Paul's desire was to advance the Gospel of the Kingdom in a way most appropriate to its success in the Roman Empire, an empire in which 2/3 of its inhabitants were slaves and in which women were considered second-class citizens at best. I am sure that if Paul were writing under the Spirit's influence today, his sanctified counsel in these areas would more accurately reflect

God's penultimate revelation in Jesus as well as the conditions prophesied regarding the New Covenant that "in
Christ there is no male nor female, slave nor free" and
that in the new age of the Spirit both "your sons and
daughters will prophesy."

The Church must listen carefully to the voice of the
Spirit as He reveals and guides us into "all truth" in our
generation. He who has an ear let him hear what the
Spirit is saying to the Church. It is for this reason that we
must never fall into the Fundamentalist trap of worshipping the Bible. We worship the Triune God who continues to speak in new and fresh ways, revealing Himself
and His will to His people. This sin of bibliolatry characterized the Pharisees of Jesus' day. The Pharisees were
Fundamentalists who believed every jot and tittle of the
written word of God and yet rejected the living Word of
God! Building monuments to God's past revelation, they
rejected God's "now" revelation in the life and ministry of
Jesus. We still have this Pharisaical spirit present with us
today. As a matter of fact, the Pharisees, like Jesus are
"the same yesterday, today and forever."

My experience with the Holy Spirit has cost me a lot
of relationships – even among family members -- and no
doubt a lot of opportunities. Men whom I once considered to be my closest friends and fathers in ministry suddenly wanted nothing to do with me. I became *persona
non grata* in places where I was formerly celebrated as the
next "big thing." Opportunities were taken away and
doors were closed, but I wouldn't trade the miraculous
movement of the Spirit I began to see in my life and min-

istry for anything in the world of religious bureaucracy. I now minister to a broader audience than ever before! I am seeing the prayer of Jesus for unity in His body become a reality. New opportunities to preach in various denominations have opened for me and I love it! I love being a Kingdom Evangelist!

In my experience, speaking in tongues is a "gateway" to the supernatural demonstrations of the Kingdom of God. It is a sign that the reign of King Jesus has been inaugurated and that all of His power and authority belong to His church. It is a powerful experience that the Lord Jesus has for every individual who loves Him and knows Him as Lord and Savior. It is for everyone. At the end of every argument against speaking in tongues, I join the Apostle Paul, "I wish that you all speak in tongues" (1Cor. 14:5).

Questions for Further Study

1. The word for salvation is *sozo*. Its meaning, according to Strong's is: to be delivered out of danger and into safety; used principally of God's rescuing believers from the penalty and power of sin – and into His provisions. It is the overall picture of salvation.

2. Look up 1 Corinthians 6:11
There are three distinct aspects of salvation found in this particular passage.

We see that the believer is washed, sanctified, and justified.

Justification carries the connotation of a legal status that declares our righteousness before a holy God. We are cleared of all charges concerning our sin. This happens at the moment of salvation.

What is the Holy Spirit's role in justification? Romans 5:1, Galatians 2:16-17, Philippians 3:9

3. The Greek word for wash refers to an entire washing – the complete removal of sin and its effects. It is a removal from within.

What is the Holy Spirit's role in this kind of washing? Ephesians 5:26, Titus 3:5

4. We also have the word sanctified. In this passage, the Greek word is *hagios* meaning to regard as set apart, consecrated, or to dedicate.

What is the Holy Spirit's role in consecration? What is the purpose? Galatians 6:14, John 17:16

5. When we talk about deliverance from demons, let's look at one more word found in the Lord's Prayer. Jesus instructs His disciples to pray that they would be delivered from evil. The word used here for deliver means to draw a person out of danger and into the deliverer. What are the connotations of this thought when Christians go through temptation or demonic torment?

"Now, don't go from this meeting and talk about tongues, but try to get people saved."

Azusa Street Revival leader, William J Seymour

CHAPTER EIGHT

The Sign of Spirit Baptism

There are several very specific reasons why speaking, praying and singing in tongues is so critically important for every Christian. The most important is because Jesus promised that for those who choose to follow Him, speaking in tongues was to be a part of their supernatural walk with Him. This should settle the issue for every believer. "These signs shall follow those who believe... they will speak with new tongues" (Mark 16:17).

There are those who resist speaking in tongues and contend it is not for them, but the clear promise of Jesus is that every Christian can and should have a consistent prayer and praise life filled with speaking, praying and singing in tongues. When a person becomes a Christian and sincerely desires to follow Jesus, the baptism in the Holy Spirit and speaking in tongues is a part of the journey.

Second, whatever others (in the world or Church) may think, when people speak in tongues, they begin to experience the reality of God's presence in a fresh and powerful way. Does this experience include the emotions? Yes. Our emotions oftentimes signal the activity of God's presence and power at work in our hearts and physical bodies in an "upon" way. When the Holy Spirit comes "upon" you, it is likely that you will feel it.

> Unbelief will, of course, dismiss all such manifestations as mere enthusiasm, there being no need to invoke the supernatural to explain them. It must indeed be granted that the emotions are radically involved in the use of tongues, just as the glands are radically involved in the exercise of love and anger. But even as the experience of love is more than glandular secretion ("a cold sweat in propinquity"), so speaking in tongues may be more than emotion. It may be emotion evoked by the presence and power of the Holy Spirit.[28]

Third, speaking in tongues enables a Christian to reach a new depth of prayer and praise. When Christians begin to pray in tongues, they find themselves free to praise, thank, adore and glorify their heavenly Father as never before. The Apostle Paul made a clear distinction between praying with the mind and allowing the Holy Spirit to pray through the Christian's human spirit. To pray with the mind is to pray prayers limited to the intellect. This is not bad. Even when praying with the mind, a Christian can be led by the Spirit through seeing visions, words of wisdom, and even words of prophecy. "Praying with the mind is sure important; God expects it of us. But through the Holy Spirit He would like to bring our prayers to completion."[29] When you pray in tongues, your voice is an expression of your spirit which is being directed by the Holy Spirit. Speaking in tongues entails the continuing control under the direction of the Holy Spirit. There is joy, elevation – but no irrationality, no lack of conscious control. There is no limit to this remarkable manifestation of the Holy Spirit and the depths of prayer it allows a Christian to experience.

If you find yourself having difficulty embracing this idea of speaking in tongues, you are not alone. Our entire Western culture has been heavily impacted by a rationalistic approach to understanding everything, including spirituality.

> Both Catholic and Protestant camps have been heavily infected by the rationalism of the Enlightenment and our Christianity has been unduly cerebral (hence its appeal to the educated only). If the Corinthians were inclined to identify the work of the Spirit with the abnormal, we tend to make the opposite mistake, and suppose that he can only manifest himself in moral renewal, spiritual illumination and through either Bible or sacraments according to our theological reference! This Attitude, however, is mere escapism from exposing ourselves to the Spirit's powerful life. He remains the Spirit of wind and fire; he remains sovereign in the church, and is not to be boxed up in any ecclesiastical compartment. It is simply not the case that healing, prophecy, exorcism and speaking in tongues died out with the last apostle.[30]

The Holy Spirit desires to enter your life in a way that transcends the rational part of your being, while not supplanting it. He wants to break out of the rigid expectations that you have for who He is and how He is supposed to operate in your life and in the life of His church. In essence, He wants for you to recognize Him as God, who is sovereignly free to do whatever He pleases even if that "rattles the cage" that You have put Him in or even causes it to implode! As the beaver says of the lion Aslan representing God in *The Lion, the Witch and the Wardrobe* when asked if Aslan is safe, "Is he safe? Of course, he is not safe, but he is good." To be clear, speaking in tongues is perfectly safe, but it may push the boundaries of your mind primarily because your mind is used to being in control. So, I ask—is your goal to experience God primarily as safe or as good in every way that He desires to be good to you? This includes praying in the language of Heaven.

Fourth, speaking, praying and singing in tongues all edify the individual Christian. "One who speaks in a tongue edifies himself..." (1Cor. 14:4). This is not in any way undesirable. The word for "edify" means to strengthen, to build up, to make more able. The question must be asked as to how tongue speech edifies either the individual or the Church. The answer is not difficult. If tongue speech is truly what it is claimed to be by the Apostle Paul, namely, the Holy Spirit speaking, praying or singing through a Christian's spirit, then it is the most basic way in which a Christian touches the supernatural presence of God in an ongoing way. One commentator says of tongues-talking, "It is a way in which the deep subconscious parts of our being can be caught up to praise the Lord; and this brings release, deep joy, peace and the longing to spend time with God in prayer which nobody who has experienced this gift will deny."[31]

Any opportunity to experience the presence of God would be edifying, for it brings confidence in the great love of God and the position the Christian holds before God along with the ability to allow the Spirit to flow through the believer at any moment. For instance, when an individual attends a meeting of the Church and a message in tongues is spoken and interpreted, this can be a powerful moment of edification. As the interpretation is released, the Holy Spirit brings to light the will of the Lord Jesus and, in doing so, speaks a specific word directed to that person. The result is wonderful. Where there was confusion and uncertainty, there is now clarity of purpose and assurance that one has heard a word from the Lord.

Corporate edification occurs as a Christian joins with the congregation in singing in tongues. Human speech is limited, but tongues speech is limitless, therefore, as the congregation sings in tongues, the Holy Spirit takes them deeper and deeper into the heart of worship and into the very presence of the Lord Jesus. Saints have reported powerful experiences of singing in tongues through the centuries; this was the greatest spiritual release at Azusa Street. Singing in tongues brings great unity to the congregation and takes the individual Christian to a new awareness of the presence of the Lord and the unique place he or she has as a child of the King!

One testimony shared in the September issue of The Apostolic Faith (the periodical produced at the Azusa Street Mission) states:

> Many have received the gift of singing as well as speaking in the inspiration of the Spirit. The Lord is giving new voices, he translates old songs into new tongues, he gives the music that is being sung by the angels and has a heavenly choir all singing the same heavenly song in harmony. It is beautiful music, no instruments are needed in the meetings.[32]

Arguments have been made, and are still being made, that a Christian who speaks in tongues is being self-centered and should turn his or her attention away from themselves and toward the Church and the world. This reasoning would appear to be unbiblical, since it is Paul who contended that interpreted tongues was equal to prophecy and insisted that "one who prophesies, edifies the Church" (1Cor. 14:4). So, if a Christian speaks, prays, or sings in tongues, she or he edifies themselves; and if they bring an interpreted message, they are, in fact, building up the Church.

This insistence on edification appears in other writings of the Apostle. Paul encouraged Christians to edify themselves and others. He stated, "...pursue the things which make for peace and the building up of one another" (Rom 14:9). The Christian is to aggressively pursue activities in the Spirit which builds up his or her spirit, and the things that build up their brothers and sisters.

The Apostle again uses the word in his *Letter to the Church at Rome,* and this time there is a demand attached. "Let each of us please his neighbor for his good, to his edification" (Rom. 15:2). "Let each of us" is an imperative. It means, do it! Regardless of the exact context in which Paul utilized the word "edification" in this passage, his commitment to activities which edify fellow believers is unmistakable.

Fifth, the Apostle Paul explained that speaking, praying and singing in tongues are desirable because it allows the Christian to enter into intercession with the aid of the Holy Spirit. "In the same way the Spirit also helps our weakness; for we do not know how to pray as we should, but the Spirit Himself intercedes for us with groanings too deep for words; and He who searches the hearts knows what the mind of the Spirit is, because He intercedes for the saints according to the will of God" (Rom. 8:26-27).

These are remarkable verses. In the midst of describing the glory with which the Christian would ultimately enter into eternity, the Apostle Paul begins to describe an aspect of eternal glory which can be experienced by the Christian now as he or she enters into intercession with the aid of the Holy Spirit. This is Charismatic prayer, or praying in tongues. Paul did not teach that the Holy Spirit was interceding for the Christian, *apart* from the Christian, but that the Spirit was constantly interceding *through* Christians. What Paul seems to have in mind is the only form of prayer left to the believer when she comes to the end of herself, frustrated with her own weakness and baffled by her ignorance of God's will. Paul declared that at that moment the Christian has absolute freedom to pray in tongues and tap into the ever-available intercessory ministry of the Holy Spirit! Great strength and spiritual courage comes from knowing that the Holy Spirit will intercede with a Christian and pray the will of God in his or her life as they seek direction, engage in spiritual warfare, pray for the release of miracles, or express any other need they may be unaware of in the natural. Timidity, doubt and fear are replaced with a boldness which no individual could possibly possess in her or his own power.

SPEAKING, PRAYING AND SINGING IN TONGUES USUALLY SERVES AS A CATALYST TO THE EXERCISE OF OTHER GIFTS...

Sixth, speaking, praying and singing in tongues usually serves as a catalyst to the exercise of other gifts and manifestations of the Holy Spirit. Immediately after the experience of speaking in tongues at Pentecost "many wonders and signs were taking place through the apostles" (Acts 2:43). Peter and John healed the lame man at the Beautiful Gate (Acts 3:1-8). "And all the more believers in the Lord, multitudes of men and women, were constantly added to their number, to such an extent that they even carried the sick out into the streets and laid them on cots and pallets, so that when Peter came by at least his shadow might fall on any one of them. Also the people from the cities in the vicinity of Jerusalem were coming together, bringing people who were sick or afflicted with unclean spirits, and they were all being healed" (Acts 5:14-16).

The gifts of miracles, words of prophecy, words of wisdom and physical healing all flow from the lives of those who speak in tongues. In this sense, the gift of tongues is a "gateway" experience.

Seventh, Paul explains that speaking, praying and singing in tongues are signs to those who have never accepted Jesus as Lord and Savior. "So then tongues are a sign, not to those who believe, but to unbelievers" (1Cor. 14:22). This is a remarkable statement, especially in light of the fact that the Church, at least the American Church, has convinced itself of the exact opposite. Among many of the most wonderfully gifted young Pentecostal and Charismatic leaders, there is an aversion to speaking in tongues out of a genuine fear that if it is allowed in the church service, it will cripple the ability of the church to reach the lost. Paul stated the opposite. He stated unequivocally that the release of the supernatural in the Church by speaking, praying and singing in tongues would be a positive sign, not to those who are Christians and do not need a sign, but to those outsiders who desperately need to experience the manifestations of the Spirit as a sign to draw them to Jesus. Of course, the Apostle expected order in the Church, but he would rebuke a cold, dead formalism and encourage, "let all things be done" (1Cor. 14:26), a command which calls for tongues as well as other charisms. If we learn anything

from history, it is that once the Church quits being em-
barrassed and ceases to apologize for the supernatural
and begins to release the gifts, including tongues, those
outside the walls of the church will be drawn by the
power of the Spirit and His awesome ability to speak to
them and meet their needs. It is not coincidental that
Pentecostal/Charismatic Christianity is experiencing explosive growth around the globe while more formal expressions of the faith plateaued and are, in most cases,
declining. Dr. R. Alan Streets writes:

> ...healings and other miracles are signs that point to
> the arrival of the Kingdom, and they validate the
> claims of the true Gospel. If we fail to see miracles in
> our churches, possibly we are not preaching the au-
> thentic gospel-the gospel of the kingdom....our theol-
> ogy often gets in the way. At an impressionable age,
> many of us (including me) were introduced to and
> embraced theological systems that explained away
> modern-day miracles, arguing that miracles ended
> when the last apostle died or the canon of Scripture
> was completed.[33]

I have witnessed the conversion of hundreds of unbelievers in response to the interpretation of a message in
tongues given in the context of Sunday morning services.
We must repent of quenching the Spirit and despising
prophetic utterances which have come to characterize so
many so-called "Spirit filled" churches in North America.

Eighth, the Apostle Paul considered praying in
tongues an essential element in the Christian's armor.
He stated, "With all prayer and petition pray at all times

in the Spirit..." (Eph. 6:18). The Greek word for "pray" in this verse is a present, middle participle and carries with it, not a demand, but an expectation that all Christians would pray in the Spirit. This expression as used by the Apostle refers to praying in tongues.[34] He voiced this expectation in the midst of itemizing the armor needed by the Christian to do battle with the enemy, namely, Satan and his demonic forces. "Take up the full armor," he demanded, "that you may be able to stand firm against the schemes of the devil" (Eph 6:13). Obviously, for the Apostle Paul, a Christian was not truly prepared for battle without an active prayer life which included praying in the language of heaven. He made this demand as strong as possible by using the second person, plural, Greek imperative. It is an all- inclusive command: "You all take up the full armor." By full armor, the Apostle meant praying in tongues! Paul seemed to imply another warfare strategy dealing with tongues. He insisted that when a Christian uses tongue speech, he or she speaks in a heavenly language that, "no one understands", then goes even further and contended that "in his spirit he speaks mysteries" (1Cor. 14:2). The Apostle saw tongues as a strategic part of the Christian armor and as a mystery language that no one understands, most especially the enemy. The Christian who is speaking in tongues is holding a secret conversation with God. It is a conversation not even the forces of hell can decode!

It is very important not to be fooled in this area. Spiritual warfare is real. The Devil is cunning. The expectation of the Apostle was explicit: the full armor included speaking, praying and singing in tongues. In fact, every critic who desires to deny the validity of tongue speech must perform hermeneutical gymnastics in order to explain away Paul's clear teaching: namely, that for the Apostle, praying in tongues is to be a part of every believer's arsenal of spiritual weaponry.

Questions for Further Study

1. Look up 1 Corinthians 14:15
The word for understanding in this passage can be translated *mind*. It encompasses the intellect, the faculty in which reason and reflective thought take place.
Paul tells us that we should pray with our mind – our intellect, but he also tells us to pray in the Spirit indicating that these are two different modes of prayer.
The word used for Spirit is *pneuma* which we studied in the first chapter.

2. What are your thoughts concerning how the Holy Spirit helps us pray with our intellect?
Why would praying in the Spirit be considered something altogether different?

3. Look up Ephesians 4:16-8
What is meant by the futility of their thinking?
Can we still have places in our understanding where we are ignorant after coming to Christ?

How would praying in the Spirit, having a Spirit led conversation with God, help us to gain wisdom?

"Do you believe in revival, my friend? Are you praying for revival? What are you trusting? Are you trusting the organizing power of the church? Or are you trusting in the power of God to pour out His Spirit upon us again, to revive us, to baptize us anew and afresh with His most blessed Holy Spirit? The church needs another Pentecost."

Dr D. Martyn Lloyd-Jones in *Joy Unspeakable*

CHAPTER NINE

So What Do I Do With All This?

I am certain that people from many different places in life will read this book. You may be in a place where you're not even ready to face death or the eternity that follows it. If you don't know that your sin is forgiven and that you are ready to face God and spend eternity in Heaven, there is good news. You can be! God wants to pour out His Holy Spirit on you and give you all of the blessings I have talked about in this book. But first, you need to receive Jesus Christ – the one who went to the cross and was tortured and who died to pay the penalty for your sins and then rose victorious over death – as Lord and Savior.

You may say, "You don't know what a sinner I am." It doesn't matter. What matters is what a fabulous Savior

Jesus is. It doesn't matter what you've done. It doesn't matter whom you've done it with. It doesn't matter where you've been. Jesus loves you so much that He shed red blood for you so that no matter what you've done, you can be forgiven and free, just like I walked out of that jail cell forgiven and free.

You Can Be Completely New!

The Bible promises you that God will fully forgive you of every sin you have ever committed when you receive Jesus Christ as Savior and Lord. Has He forgiven you? Have you called on the name of the Lord? Have you received Jesus as Lord and Savior? Are you saved? Do you know for sure that your sins are forgiven? If you were to die today, are you certain that you would spend eternity in heaven with the Lord Jesus? Are you ready to meet Him?

If not, today can be the day of your salvation. Call out to Him today. Pray in your own words, admit that you are a sinner, that you believe that Jesus died for you to pay the price for your sins and that He's alive. Tell Him that you accept His forgiveness and mercy and that the best you know how, you will turn from your sin and begin to walk with Him from this day forward.

If you are now trusting Christ, the Bible has very good news for you! The Bible clearly states that "everyone who calls on the name of the Lord shall be saved" (Rom. 10:13). You can have absolute assurance that you are forgiven, clean and prepared to face eternity, because God Himself promises to forgive you and save you.

Whether you have just received Jesus as Lord and Savior while reading this book or have walked with Him for many years, God wants to pour the Holy Spirit out upon you. He wants to baptize you, to completely immerse you, in the Holy Spirit and to fill you with the love and power of Jesus so that you can tell the world about Him.

> *GOD WANTS TO POUR THE HOLY SPIRIT OUT UPON YOU. HE WANTS TO BAPTIZE YOU, TO COMPLETELY IMMERSE YOU, IN THE HOLY SPIRIT AND TO FILL YOU WITH THE LOVE AND POWER OF JESUS SO THAT YOU CAN TELL THE WORLD ABOUT HIM.*

Call upon Jesus today – right now – and ask Him in your own words to fill you to overflowing with the Holy Spirit. Ask Him to baptize you in the Holy Spirit in the same way He baptized His earliest followers on the Day of Pentecost and continues to do to this very hour. Open your mouth and begin to pray, praise and worship God in the new language He will give you. Don't be afraid of the Holy Spirit. You might simply say, "Father I want everything which You have for me." Then, by faith, receive this empowerment. You may or may not have overwhelming feelings or a heightened emotional reaction. Remember, it is the "filling" of the Spirit and not the "feeling" of the Spirit which you desire.

In the end, while speaking in tongues is part of the experience of being filled with the Holy Spirit, being filled with the Holy Spirit isn't just about speaking in tongues. It is about being filled with the power and presence of the Holy Spirit. It's about having the same burden for those who have never received Jesus as Lord and Savior. It's about being filled with His power and His love so that you can effectively reach others with the love and forgiveness of Jesus. "In recapturing the dynamic life of the Spirit there will...be the renewal of the charismata (or spiritual gifts), not for the sake of being charismatic, but for the building up of the people of God for their life together and in the world."[35]

Perhaps as you are reading, the Spirit has convicted you that you have lost your burden for those who have never received Jesus. You have become more interested in judging people for their sins than telling them the good news that Jesus has paid the price for their sins and loves them no matter what bondage they are in at the moment. This may be hard to read, but you need to hear it: If you do not have a burden for the lost, you need to go before the Lord and ask Him to break your heart. If you are saved and you are not an active witness for Jesus in this world, something is very wrong. There are really only two types of Christians: soul winners and backsliders. Jesus said that if we follow Him, He will make us become fishers of men. If you're not fishing, then you're not following. You need a fresh infilling of the Spirit whether you speak in tongues already or not. You need a fresh empowering, a fresh encounter with Jesus. Ask

God to fill you afresh and anew. He will do it if you will get real with Him and ask.

Wherever you are in your walk with Jesus, God wants to pour out the Holy Spirit upon you in a fresh and powerful way daily. When you allow that to take place, you will change. Your prayer life will become critically important to you. The Bible will become more than black ink on white paper. There will be a new desire to love and worship the Lord Jesus. Your eyes will be open to those in need around you and new opportunities to share the love of Jesus with others will fill your life. You'll become less judgmental and more gracious. You will begin to walk in a new supernatural power and anointing. You will sense a new surge of faith rising up within you to step out and believe God for miracles in your life and in the lives of others. The presence of the Holy Spirit will be obvious. You will begin to hear Him speak to you in very personal ways. You will touch the miraculous and see great demonstrations of the ministry of the Spirit in your life. Like Jesus said, you will receive power when the Holy Spirit comes upon you and you will be His witness.

Lord Jesus, pour out the Holy Spirit on your Church!

Notes

[1] Stetzer, Ed and Mike Dodson, Comeback Churches (Nashville, Tennessee: B & H Publishing Group, 2007), ix.

[2] According to a Pew Forum study conducted in 2011, there were approximately 584,080,000 "Pentecostals" and "Charismatics" in the world. http://www.pewforum.org/2011/12/19/global-christianity-movements-and-denominations/ [accessed March 31, 2016].

[3] McDowell, Josh and Bob Hostetler, Right From Wrong: What You Need To Know To Help Youth Make Right Choices (Dallas, Texas: Word Publishing, 1994), 8.

[4] Gordon D. Fee, *God's Empowering Presence: The Holy Spirit in the Letters of Paul* (Peabody, MA: Hendrickson Publishers, 2005), 894-895.

[5] Clark Pinnock, "Baptists and the 'Latter Rain': A Contemporary Challenge and Hope for Tomorrow," pp. 255-272 in Costly Vision: The Baptist Pilgrimage in Canada, ed. Jarold K. Zeaman (Burlington, ON: Welch, 1988), 266.

[6] John Calvin, The Institutes of the Christian Religion (Inst., 1.3.1)

[7] The R.C. Sproul Ed., *The Reformation Study Bible* (Lake Mary, Florida: Ligonier Ministries, 2005), 1783.

[8] Ibid. The commentary states concerning "the elementary doctrine of Christ" (mentioned in verse 1) that these teachings, the ones that are enumerated in verses 1 and 2, are the ABC's of Christian doctrine. All of these doctrines can be found in *The Book of Acts.*

[9] This is not to dismiss the fact there are many who may come to faith through dreams and visions apart from the immediate action of the Church.

[10] Several works have traced the use of tongues (among the other gifts of the Spirit) throughout Church history. See Stanley M. Burgess, *The Spirit and the Church: Ancient Christian Traditions* (Peabody, MA: Hendrickson Publishers, 1990) and Ronald A. N. Kydd, *Charismatic Gifts in the Early Church: The Gifts of the Spirit in the First 300 Years* (Peabody, MA: Hendrickson Publishers, 2014).

[11] Gordon D. Fee, *God's Empowering Presence: The Holy Spirit in the Letters of Paul* (Peabody, MA: Hendrickson Publishers, 2005), p. 585.

[12] Frank Bartleman, *Azusa Street* (South Plainfield, NJ: Bridge Publishing, 1980), xviii.

[13] Conrad Gempf, *NIV Application Commentary* (Zondervan, Grand Rapids, MI 1998), 90-91.

[14] Luke lists those present as: "Parthians and Medes and Elamites, and residents of Mesopotamia, Judea and Cappadocia, Pontus and Asia, Phrygia and Pamphylia, Egypt and the districts of Libya around Cyrene, and visitors from Rome, both Jews and proselytes, Cretans and Arabs – we hear them in our own tongues speaking the might deeds of God (Acts 2:9-11)."

[15] Thomas C. Oden, *Life in the Spirit* in Systematic Theology 3 (San Francisco: Harper, San Francisco, 1992), 47.

[16] See Gary B. McGee, Initial Evidence: Historical and Biblical Perspectives on the Pentecostal Doctrine of Spirit Baptism (Peabody, MA: Hendrickson Publishers, 1991); and Robert P. Menzies, Speaking in Tongues: Jesus and the Apostolic Church as Models for the Church Today (Cleveland, TN: CPT Press, 2016).

[17] Francis A. Schaeffer, *No Little People* (Wheaton, 2003), 66.

[18] W. J. Conybeare and J. S. Howson, The Life and Epistles of St. Paul, (Grand Rapids: Eerdmans, 2004), 67. "The Jews in Damascus were very numerous; and there were peculiar circumstances in the political condition of Damascus which may have given facilities to conspiracies or deeds of violence conducted by the Jews."

[19] Robert P. Menzies and William W. Menzies, *Spirit and Power: Foundations of Pentecostal Experience* (Grand Rapids, MI: Zondervan Publishing House, 2000), 3.

[20] Pentecostal scholar John Wyckoff offers a paradigm-shifting view of the purpose of speaking tongues within the church service. He contests the idea that tongues-speech, particularly when interpreted, is a form of prophecy (which is the way traditional Pentecostals have viewed it). Instead, he asserts that the Spirit inspires believers within the context of the local congregation to pray or praise in tongues primarily for the purpose of personal edification yet in a corporate context. Thus, instead of a single believer speaking in tongues and another believer interpreting the unintelligible message for the corporate body, many believers speak or sing in tongues simultaneously as an expression of devotion or petition to God. This corporate expression of worship, in order to be biblical, would still need to be interpreted, but the content of that interpretation would be prayer or praise instead of a prophetic message. In this way, a church can enjoy a version of its own Acts 2 Pentecost experience, during which the participants were said to be speaking of "the mighty works of God". See Contemporary Issues in Pneumatology: Festschrift in Honor of George M. Flattery, Edited by James E. Richardson, Global University, Springfield, MO, 2009 for more about this view.

[21] Frank Macchia, *Justified in the Spirit* (Grand Rapids, MI: Eerdmans, 2010), 118.

[22] Roger Stronstad, *The Charismatic Theology of St. Luke* (Peabody, MA: Hendrickson Publishers: 2005), 80.

[23] Frank Macchia, *Justified in the Spirit* (Grand Rapids, MI: Eerdmans, 2010), 259.

[24] Frank Macchia, *Justified in the Spirit* (Grand Rapids, MI: Eerdmans, 2010), 97-98.

[25] Larry McQueen, Joel and the Spirit: The Cry of a Prophetic Hermeneutic (Cleveland, TN: CPT Press, 2009), p.???. Also, see the many papers presented at the Society for Pentecostal Studies annual meeting in 1999 covering the topic: "Toward Healing Our Divisions: Reflecting on Diversity and Common Witness".

[26] John MacArthur, Strange Fire (Nashville: Thomas Nelson, 2013), 154.

[27] Daniel Crabtree, "An Examination of 1 Timothy 2:8-15," which is adapted from his doctoral project "Let Them Preach: A Class on Women in Ministry" (2006) republished with permission by http://wim.ag.org/0703/0703_1timothy2_8_15.cfm [accessed March 31, 2016]. For a similar conclusion, see, Gordon Fee, 1 and 2 Timothy (San Francisco, CA: Harper Row Publishers, 1984), pp. 33-40, and Craig S. Keener, Paul, Women & Wives: Marriage and Women's Ministry in the Letters of Paul (Peabody, MA: Hendrickson Publishers, 1992).

[28] This statement was made by the late Paul K Jewett, long time distinguished Professor of Theology at Fuller Seminary and quoted in the Zondervan Pictorial Encyclopedia of the Bible Vol. 3 (Grand Rapids, MI: Zondervan Publishing House, 1975), 192.

[29] J. Rodman Williams, Renewal Theology: Systematic Theology from a Charismatic Perspective: Three Volumes in One (Grand Rapids, MI: Zondervan, 1996), in loc.

[30] Michael Green, I Believe in the Holy Spirit (Grand Rapids, MI: Eerdmans, 1980), 197-98).

[31] Ibid, 199.

[32] The Apostolic Faith 1.1 (Sept. 1906), 1. This became a regular feature of Pentecostal experience that was testified to in numerous issues of this periodical.

[33] Dr. R. Alan Street, Heaven on Earth: Experiencing the Kingdom of God in the Here and Now (Eugene, Oregon: Harvest House, 2013), 123.

---

[34] J. Rodman Williams contends that because the language is so similar to Paul's message about tongues to the Corinthians, this text clearly indicates praying in tongues by the use of "in the Spirit" even though he clarifies this would not be all that would be entailed, *Renewal Theology: Systematic Theology from a Charismatic Perspective: Three Volumes in One* (Grand Rapids, MI: Zondervan, 1996), 218.

[35] Gordon D. Fee, *God's Empowering Presence: The Holy Spirit in the Letters of Paul* (Peabody, MA: Hendrickson Publishers, 2005), 902.

Sources

Bartleman, Frank. Azusa Street. South Plainfield, NJ: Bridge Publishing, 1980.

Burgess, Stanley M. The Spirit and the Church: Ancient Christian Traditions. Peabody, MA: Hendrickson Publishers, 1990.

Calvin, John. The Institutes of the Christian Religion.

Conybeare, W. J. and J. S. Howson. The Life and Epistles of St. Paul. Grand Rapids, MI: Eerdmans, 2004

Crabtree, Daniel. "An Examination of 1 Timothy 2:8-15," (adapted from his doctoral project "Let Them Preach: A Class on Women in Ministry,"), 2006.

Fee, Gordon D. 1 and 2 Timothy. San Francisco, CA: Harper Row Publishers, 1984.

Fee, Gordon D. God's Empowering Presence: The Holy Spirit in the Letters of Paul. Peabody, MA: Hendrickson Publishers, 2005.

Gempf, Conrad. NIV Application Commentary. Grand Rapids, MI: Zondervan, 1998.

Green, Michael. I Believe in the Holy Spirit. Grand Rapids, MI: Eerdmans, 1980.

Jewett, Paul K. Zondervan Pictorial Encyclopedia of the Bible, Vol. 3. Grand Rapids, MI: Zondervan Publishing House, 1975.

Keener, Craig S. Paul, Women & Wives: Marriage and Women's Ministry in the Letters of Paul. Peabody, MA: Hendrickson Publishers, 1992.

Kydd, Ronald A. N. Charismatic Gifts in the Early Church: The Gifts of the Spirit in the First 300 Years. Peabody, MA: Hendrickson Publishers, 2014.

MacArthur, John. Strange Fire. Nashville: Thomas Nelson, 2013.

Macchia, Frank. Justified in the Spirit. Grand Rapids, MI: Eerdmans, 2010.

McDowell, Josh and Bob Hostetler. Right From Wrong: What You Need To Know To Help Youth Make Right Choices. Dallas, TX: Word Publishing, 1994.

McGee, Gary B. Initial Evidence: Historical and Biblical Perspectives on the Pentecostal Doctrine of Spirit Baptism. Peabody, MA: Hendrickson Publishers, 1991.

McQueen, Larry. Joel and the Spirit: The Cry of a Prophetic Hermeneutic. Cleveland, TN: CPT Press, 2009.

Menzies, Robert P. Speaking in Tongues: Jesus and the Apostolic Church as Models for the Church Today. Cleveland, TN: CPT Press, 2016.

Menzies, Robert P. and William W. Menzies. Spirit and Power: Foundations of Pentecostal Experience. Grand Rapids, MI: Zondervan Publishing House, 2000.

Oden, Thomas C. Life in the Spirit in Systematic Theology 3. San Francisco: Harper, 1992.

Pinnock, Clark. "Baptists and the 'Latter Rain': A Contemporary Challenge and Hope for Tomorrow," in Costly Vision: The Baptist Pilgrimage in Canada, Jarold K. Zeaman, ed. Burlington, ON: Welch, 1988.

Schaeffer, Francis A. No Little People. Wheaton: Crossway Books, 2003.

Sproul, R. C., Ed. <u>The Reformation Study Bible</u>. Lake Mary, Florida: Ligonier Ministries, 2005.

Stetzer, Ed, and Mike Dodson. <u>Comeback Churches</u>. Nashville, TN: B & H Publishing Group, 2007.

Streett, Dr. R. Alan. <u>Heaven on Earth: Experiencing the Kingdom of God in the Here and Now</u>. Eugene, Oregon: Harvest House, 2013.

Stronstad, Roger. <u>The Charismatic Theology of St. Luke</u>. Peabody, MA: Hendrickson Publishers, 2005.

Williams, J. Rodman. <u>Renewal Theology: Systematic Theology from a Charismatic Perspective: Three Volumes in One</u>. Grand Rapids, MI: Zondervan, 1996.

Journals, Conferences, Websites

Pew Forum website. article, Global Christianity Movements And Denominations. http://www.pewforum.org/2011/12/19/global-christianity-movements-and-denominations/ , 2011.

Society for Pentecostal Studies. "Toward Healing Our Divisions: Reflecting on Diversity and Common Witness." 1999.

The Apostolic Faith 1.1. September, 1906.

Suggested Reading

Deere, Jack. Surprised by the Power of the Spirit. Grand Rapids, MI: Zondervan, 1993.

Dunn, James D. G. Baptism in the Holy Spirit. Philadelphia, PA: The Westminster Press, 1977.

Ervin, Howard M. Conversion-Initiation and the Baptism in the Holy Spirit. Peabody, MA: Hendrickson Publishers, 1985.

Grudem, Wayne. The Gift of Prophecy in the New Testament and Today. Wheaton, IL: Crossway Books, 1988.

Lloyd-Jones, D. Martin. Joy Unspeakable. Wheaton, IL: Shaw Books, 2000.

Menzies, Robert. Empowered for Witness: The Spirit in Luke-Acts. New York, NY: T & T Clark International, A Continuum Imprint, 1995.

Moreland, J. P. Kingdom Triangle. Grand Rapids, MI: Zondervan, 1994.

Oss, Doug. Are Miraculous Gifts for Today? Grand Rapids, MI: Zondervan, 1996.

Packer, J. I. Keep in Step with the Spirit. Grand Rapids, MI: Baker Books, 1984.

Pinnock, Clark H. Flame of Love: A Theology of the Holy Spirit. Downers Grove, IL: InterVarsity Press, 1996.

Sherrill, John. They Speak with Other Tongues. Grand Rapids, MI: Chosen Books, 2004.

Stott, John R. W. <u>Baptism and Fullness: The Work of the Holy Spirit Today</u>. Downers Grove, IL: InterVarsity Press, 1964.

Williams, J. Rodman. <u>Renewal Theology</u>. Grand Rapids, MI: Zondervan Publishing House, 1996.

About the Author

Dr. Scott Camp has a unique blend of life experiences that give him a powerful relevant ministry to reach the unreachable with the message of Christ. He was the product of a teenage pregnancy, alcoholism, and a broken home. His own drug and alcohol abuse led to a felony charge and he was arrested while in high school. It was there that Scott committed his life to following Christ and shortly thereafter was called to preach. Dr. Camp has served in a variety of capacities since entering vocational ministry in 1982, including student pastor, evangelist, church planter, college professor, and Dean of

Students. He has been the Sr. Pastor of four growing congregations which include First Baptist Church of Sachse, TX; Metro Church of Garland, TX; First Baptist Church of Mansfield, TX; and most recently, Fellowship of Joy in Grand Prairie, TX.

Dr. Camp now travels extensively throughout the United States, Eastern Europe, Mexico, South America, Pakistan and the continent of Africa preaching at churches, city-wide crusades, and conferences. He has been featured as a program guest with the Billy Graham Crusade. Dr. Camp currently serves as the Faculty Chair of Evangelism at SUM Bible College and Theological Seminary in Oakland, CA

Thousands have responded to the gospel under his ministry worldwide. He has ministered to international audiences in person as well as via television and radio broadcasts. His ministry has been covered in various newspaper magazine articles including the Dallas Morning News and Ft. Worth Star Telegram. He has also preached at numerous state evangelism conferences, youth evangelism conference, and pastor's conferences across the nation for various denominational and inter-denominational groups.

Dr. Camp holds a Masters of Arts in Theology from Criswell College, where he graduated Summa Cum Laude. In addition, he holds a Master of Divinity from Southwestern Assemblies of God University and a Master of Theology Degree from Southwestern Baptist Theological Seminary. In 2007, he was awarded an honorary Doctor of Divinity from St. Thomas Christian College in

Jacksonville, FL. He is currently completing the Doctor of Ministry program at Assemblies of God Theological Seminary in Springfield, MO.

Scott married his wife, Gina in 1988 and they have four children: Sarah, Dillon, Joshua, and Madison. Gina has taught music, directed children's choirs and has also been a featured vocalist and worship leader at various conferences.

If you would like more information about Scott or if you are interested in contacting him to see about having a harvest crusade or Friend Day in your church, then check out his website.

www.ScottCamp.org

The goal of Franklin Publishing is to enable Pastors, Evangelists, and Christian leaders and presenters to become published authors. Becoming a published author expands your influence and builds your ministry. You can write the book or sermon series which God has laid on your heart. We can walk that road with you.

www.FranklinPublishing.org

CPSIA information can be obtained
at www.ICGtesting.com
Printed in the USA
LVOW13s2350160318
570065LV00002BA/3/P